THE 18TH CENTURY ENSLAVING INDUSTRY

LANCASTER QUAKERS' INVOLVEMENT

What people are saying about

The 18th Century Enslaving Industry - Lancaster Quakers' Involvement

Dr Rhiannon Grant – Woodbrooke College's Deputy Programme Leader for Research and Programme Coordinator for Modern Quaker Thought.

This important book brings to the fore the ways in which a local study can speak to complex world events. By tracing the lives and families of Lancaster Quakers who were involved in trading enslaved people and goods produced using slave labour, Ann Morgan shows how these immoral and unjust practices were deeply intertwined with normal society and charitable giving. Understanding the nuanced truth of this history as a source of present injustice is a vital step in creating a more equitable society today, and this book will be helpful to British Quakers, members of other churches, social justice campaigners, and others concerned with repairing these harms.

Professor Alan Rice, Director Institute for Black Atlantic Research, University of Central Lancashire.

Ann Morgan's book sheds a much-needed light on the activities of Eighteenth Century Lancaster Quakers in the business of slavery. From slave ship owners and captains to West Indian Merchants, from plantation owners to dealers in goods made by enslaved Africans, Lancaster Quakers were involved in all aspects of the trade. As well as detailing the family interconnections that implicated so many of them, Morgan also painstakingly shows how the instructions from the London meeting after 1761 to fully investigate these activities were ignored so that although many were disowned by the Lancaster Meeting for other activities over this period not one of the 18 most obviously implicated were sanctioned in any way for their dealings in the slavery business. Morgan skilfully navigates the family and business connections of generations of Lancaster Quakers to create the definitive resource for understanding how Quakers so much known for abolition elsewhere had a very different and shameful legacy in Lancaster.

Dr Nicholas Radburn, author of 'Traders in Men: Merchants and the Transformation of the Transatlantic Slave Trade'

For centuries, Quakers have been lauded as foresighted abolitionists who decisively hastened the ending of Britain's slave trade. Through her detailed study of Lancaster families who were engaged in every aspect of the "slavery business," Ann Morgan reveals a much darker side to Quakerism. Lancaster Quakers, she shows, traded and owned enslaved people, bought and sold slave-grown commodities, and manufactured goods for the slave economy. As Morgan demonstrates, the Lancaster Quaker meeting tacitly accepted the engagement of its members in the slavery business despite precepts to the contrary. These explosive findings are soundly founded on deep and robust research. This is, hence, a book that will spark much soul-searching amongst Quakers across the globe while also appealing to scholars and general readers who want to better understand Britain's deep entanglements with Atlantic slavery.

THE 18TH CENTURY ENSLAVING INDUSTRY

LANCASTER QUAKERS' INVOLVEMENT

Copyright © Ann Morgan 2025

The right of Ann Morgan to be identified as the author of this work has been attested by her in accordance with the Copyright, Designs and Patents Act 1988

CONTENT

Chapters   Page

foreword	6
Introduction	7
Lancaster Quaker Merchants In The 17th & 18th Centuries	18
The Lawson Families	23
Young Men Who Came To Lancaster To Make Their Fortunes	34
The Satterthwaite; Townson; Dillworth & Rawlinson Families	43
The Dillworth Families	47
The Satterthwaite Families	53
The Rawlinson Families	63
Colonial Traders	94
Lancaster Monthly Meeting	108
Quakers Outside Lancashire Who Supplied The Industry	113
Why Is This History Important?	119
Appendix 1	121
Section Vi - Slavery And The Slave Trade	121
Timeline	122
Portraits	129
Glossary	132
The Author	136
Acknowledgements	137
Index	138

Foreword

This book uncovers a little-known history of Quakers in Britain. It demonstrates how the activities of a group of Lancaster Quaker Merchants involved in the enslaving industry fitted the accepted social, political and moral attitudes of 17th and 18th century Britain towards the enslavement of Africans. It suggests that the single heroic narrative of British Quakers being abolitionists masks the truth that some British Quakers were heavily involved in all aspects of the enslaving industry and that despite Quakers centrally opposing enslaving, they were not formally challenged or disowned.

The use of family histories to follow the fortunes of these men whilst providing an insight into the early Quaker movement explains how the money generated by enslaving Africans came back into British society to finance infrastructure projects such as canals, turnpikes and country houses to establish banks and cotton mills supporting the development of the industrial revolution, to provide community welfare projects and enhanced social status for the families. These families present a picture of what was happening to many of the families of the 13,000 people in Britain who invested in the enslaving industry. Their money made a major contribution to building the society in which we live and from which we benefit today at the expense of the labour and lives of past enslaved Africans.

It is hoped that this guide will support future researchers as these historical and ongoing injustices are investigated and brought into the light.

Introduction

Recognising honestly our history, that the Transatlantic Chattel Slave Trade was pivotal to the development of Britain in the 18th and 19th centuries and a source of European white privilege and wealth, is crucial to our understanding of the position and experiences of people of African descent and 21st century Britain. The Transatlantic Chattel Slave Trade reordered society, changed the demography of Africa, South and Southern America and the West Indies, changed the economy of Britain and left a legacy of racism, stereotypes and white supremacy in British society that will, in all probability, take longer to eradicate than the 145 years it took to abolish the enslavement industry in the British Empire.

Quakers, who are rightly known for their involvement in the abolition of enslavement movement, were involved in enslaving. That is the other side of Quaker history. This book asks and sets out to identify, as far as it is possible, a truthful answer to the following questions:
How involved were individual members of Lancaster Quaker Monthly Meeting in the enslaving industry, including the trafficking of enslaved people and their ownership on plantations?
Which Lancaster Quakers oiled the wheels of this industry by importing, manufacturing and selling goods the enslaved were forced to produce during the 17th, 18th & 19th Centuries?
How did the wealth from the enslaving industry change the lives of those involved and contribute to the privileged society in which we in Britain live today?

The Quaker Testimony to Truth requires Friends (Quakers) to know, accept and acknowledge this story which has not been brought fully into the light by those who have written in the past about numerous aspects of the life of early Lancaster and district Friends. The Maritime Museum in Lancaster highlights Lancaster's part in the enslaving industry, naming three Quakers involved. This study identifies significantly more and is an attempt to repair and face that part of Lancaster and district Quaker history.

The root of the Transatlantic Chattel Slave Trade goes back to 1325 and the arrival of Genoese traders in the Canaries, followed by Portuguese and Spanish expeditions. A Papal Bull of 1403 classified the natives of the Canaries as infidels, which made them liable for enslavement and allowed them to be traded.

In the Canaries, the Spanish set up a system that was to provide a model for future slave trading, whilst the Portuguese found a system of enslaving well established by Africans further south. By 1450, trade in enslaved Africans had become Portugal's most profitable commerce with Africa.

To protect Portuguese trade rights, King Afonso V of Portugal appealed to Pope Nicholas V for support, seeking the moral authority of the Church for his monopoly. The Papal Bull of 1452 was addressed to Afonso V. A translated extract reads:

'We grant you by these present documents, with our Apostolic Authority, full and free permission to invade, search out, capture and subjugate the Saracens and pagans and any other unbelievers and enemies of Christ wherever they may be, as well as their kingdoms, duchies, counties, principalities, and other property [...] and to reduce their persons into perpetual servitude.'

This marked the beginning of the Doctrine of Discovery. A subsequent Papal Bull on the 13th of March, 1456, reaffirmed the first. It recognised Portugal's rights to the territories it had discovered along the West African coast and the 'reduction of the infidels and non-Christian territories to perpetual vassals' of the Christian monarch.

In 1493, Pope Alexander VI issued a Papal Bull, "Inter Caetera," in which he authorised Spain and Portugal to colonise the Americas and its native peoples as subjects. The decree asserted the rights of Spain and Portugal to colonise, convert and enslave. It justified the enslavement of Africans.

'We [therefore] weighing all and singular the premises with due meditation and noting that since we had formerly by other letters of ours granted among other things free and ample faculty to the aforesaid King Alfonso -- to invade, search out, capture, vanquish, and subdue all Saracens and pagans whatsoever, and other enemies of Christ wheresoever placed, and the kingdoms, dukedoms, principalities, dominions, possessions, and all movable and immovable goods whatsoever held and possessed by them and to reduce their persons to perpetual slavery, and to apply and appropriate to himself and his successors the kingdoms, dukedoms, counties, principalities, dominions, possessions, and goods, and to convert them to his and their use and profit.' [1]

These Papal Bulls established a spiritual, political and legal justification for the colonisation and seizure of land not inhabited by Christians and the perpetual enslavement of non-Christians.

Colonisation and enslavement of non-Christians were seen not only in Portuguese and Spanish society as just activities from the 15th century but also in other European countries, including Britain.

The Canon Law of the Catholic Church, adopted by the Anglican community on the disestablishment of the Catholic Church in 1534, identified African people as physically, psychologically and theologically inferior.

The conflict between Spain and Portugal, settled by a treaty, gave Portugal a sphere of influence in Sub-Saharan Africa that effectively cut Spain off from the main supply of enslaved Africans. The treaty, drafted prior to the discover of the Americas in 1492, left both able to claim rights to the Americas. The Papacy acted as arbitrator and issued two new bulls in 1493, dividing the Atlantic world between the two Iberian powers. These were only renounced in the 'Joint statement of the Dicasteries for Culture and Education and for Promoting Integral Human Development on the 'Doctrine of Discovery'' issued by Pope Francis and published by the Vatican on the 30th of March 2023. Thus the 'Doctrine of Discovery' was in existence for 550 years.

The opportunities that the 'Doctrine of Discovery' offered were embraced by other European countries, including Britain, and underpinned attitudes towards enslavement across 17th & 18th century British society. By this time, the exploitation of people in West Africa as slaves and free labour had been developing for 200 years with the Papacy as arbitrator. It had become an entirely acceptable process to establish the new economies in the Caribbean and across the Americas both north and south. [2]

British royalty became involved. For example, Queen Elizabeth I sponsored the voyage of John Hawkins in 1562. He traded enslaved people from Sierra Leone to the American plantations, trading them for hides, pearls and sugar. Elizabeth even gave him a unique coat of arms bearing a bonded slave and took a portion of the profit. In 1660, King Charles II granted a charter to the Company of Royal Adventurers Trading to Africa. Led by the king's younger brother, the Duke of York (later King James II), this group had a monopoly on British trade with West Africa, including gold, silver and the enslaved. The original company collapsed under mounting debts in 1667 but re-emerged in 1672 with a new royal charter and a new name: the Royal African Company (RAC). They partnered in 1711 with the South Sea Company specifically to trade 4,800 enslaved Africans, healthy men, annually for 30 years to Spanish colonies in the New World.

Thus, when the Quaker Church was established in Britain in 1652, trading in people from Africa had become the norm. By the end of the 17th century, England led the world in trading enslaved people from West Africa, making full use of the infrastructure that the Portuguese and Spanish had developed. England would continue to lead this industry throughout the 18th century. It is estimated that this economic activity represented 11% of British GDP during the 18th century. The number of enslaved Africans Britain transported to its colonies between 1640 and 1807 was 3.1 million, accounting for 50% of all enslaved Africans kidnapped and transported during that period. About 2.7 million are thought to have survived the gruelling journey known as the "middle passage" and were forcibly resettled in the Caribbean, North and South America, and elsewhere. It was the largest forced migration in human history placing race at the centre of reorganising and stratifying the global economy and society. [3]

Early Quakers were amongst those colonising areas of America. William Penn, in 1680, received a patent from Charles II for a tract of land in America that he established as Pennsylvania and in 1698, twenty Lancaster Quakers sold their land and goods. They left with their families to sail via Liverpool on the *Britannia* to settle in Pennsylvania.

During this period, there were at least thirteen thousand people in Britain investing in the Transatlantic Slave Trade out of a population of ten million. [4] It was not just a commercial elite. Most of the investors were looking to enhance their social and business standing in their community. Some were immigrants. Many were small and medium size investors who had a little money surplus to their day-to-day financial needs. Small business owners such as butchers, rope makers, fishmongers, victuallers and shoemakers are amongst over 100 occupations listed on the Slave Trader Register in 2024 (a cross institutional initiative between Lancaster University, the University of Manchester and University College London's Centre for the Study of Legacies of British Slavery). They invested anything between £1 and £200 (the equivalent of £186 - £31,171 in 2024, according to the Bank of England's historic Inflation rate calculator). This money financed the industry itself and the trading posts and forts on the West coast of Africa built to house captured Africans waiting for embarkation. The enslaving industry did not guarantee a profit. In fact, a good number did not make any money from their investments as ships, and their cargos, were in danger of capture or shipwreck. For those who did, it provided the wealth to improve their social standing, build their businesses, display their wealth in the form of beautiful houses, dress differently as gentlemen, ensure a good education for their male offspring, marry off their daughters well, often to enhance their business prospects and to contribute to the built environment in their localities. It enabled welfare buildings such as hospitals and education establishments to be built and for welfare projects looking after the poor of a parish to be established. It helped to prime Britain's industrial revolution.

Africa was also changed as the enslaving industry expanded in the 18th century, and demand for the enslaved increased. Professor James Walvin explains that the African states, which for centuries had enslaved their enemies, now captured far more prisoners than before. They sold such persons to traders from Europe. The African Merchants received in payment from British traders' textiles, beads, substandard firearms which had been rejected by the British Ordnance Office, gunpowder, which became known as 'Africa power or Liverpool gold' and cowrie shells (used as currency). [5]

The continuing industry encouraged African tribes to take more of their enemies subjugated in war into enslavement, resulting in more fighting on the continent. The removal of thousands of able-bodied men into enslavement and transportation changed the demography of the West Coast African nations as well as of the countries to which they were transported.

These African traders who brought the enslaved down to the coastal trading posts were generally astute. They had regional preferences and tastes in what payment they would accept which were recognised and catered for by the British traders. For example, Indian cotton was in great demand in the Cameroons, beads were in demand in Angola, and gunpowder in The Gambia, New Calabar, the Windward Coast and Bonny.

The Lancaster Quakers involved were not exceptions. Rather, they were versions of us in a different time and circumstances. They were part of a national industry that was started in London and supported by the monarchy. It spread out to the West coast ports of Bristol, Liverpool, Lancaster, Whitehaven and Glasgow. In all, enslaving ships sailed from 23 British ports with goods to exchange for human beings. They were part of a system that created two classes of human beings and allowed one to enslave the other.

In **1676,** George Fox (the founder of the Quaker movement) reminded Friends of the human dignity of enslaved Africans after his visit to Barbados in 1671, where he saw the plight of the enslaved labourers. He wrote:

'…if you were in the same condition as the Blacks are… now I say, if this should be the condition of you and yours, you would think it hard measure, yea, and very great Bondage and Cruelty. And therefore, consider seriously of this, and do you for and to them, as you would willingly have them or any other to do unto you… were you in the like slavish condition and bring them to know the Lord Christ.'

Whilst in Barbados, he had not called for an end to slavery as a practice. He had urged Friends to provide time for the enslaved to worship, to provide them with a Christian education, to treat them well and to introduce them to Quakerism, to ensure they were law-abiding. He did not, however, envisage a shared Meeting for Worship for the Quaker household and their enslaved. [6] Fox was concerned with their spiritual lives, that they should be offered spiritual equality before God.

Fox's letter of 1671 to the Governor of Barbados reassured the authorities that far from inciting the enslaved to rebel, Friends were teaching them 'to be sober and to fear God, and to love their masters and mistresses and to be faithful and diligent in their masters' service and business'. [7]

Stuart Masters, in the 2020 Salter Lecture 'Heaven on Earth', given during the Quakers in Britain Yearly Meeting, explored how radical first-generation Quaker's beliefs were seen as threatening to the rigid order of the day and how Quakers adapted in subsequent generations to be accepted by a wider society. He explains that in a society where they were 'enemy number one' and were being 'arrested in large numbers' in order to survive, within a generation they had moved from their radical view that social inequality was a product of fallen humanity. By 1678, some Quakers were saying that social orders were divinely ordained and that social inequality was no longer a sin but what God intended. 'It is quite shocking,' he says, 'that George Fox finds a way to justify slavery in the form of a covenant slavery, that is, the idea that a slave will be part of a family, treated well and released after a certain time.' This, Master argues, was Fox's way to justify Quakers being involved in slave-based economies.

There was an unquestioning acceptance in Britain of trading in the enslaved. This developed into a culturally engrained bias against black people who were seen as socially and spiritually inferior. That bias remains to this day in the form of racism which is systemic in some institutions in British society. Quaker Merchants who either sold goods produced by the enslaved, engaged in the Transatlantic Chattel Slave Trade or owned the enslaved on plantations were all contributing to the development of this bias and current British racism.

When the London Yearly Meeting in 1727 publicly denounced slavery, they were really questioning what had become accepted practice in British society and the colonies. They were dissenting.

LONDON YEARLY MEETING & MEETING FOR SUFFERINGS' VIEWS ON THE ENSLAVEMENT INDUSTRY

In **1727**, Quakers used the London Yearly Meeting publicly to censor the enslaving industry.

'It is the sense of this meeting that the importation of negroes from their native country and relations by Friends is not a commendable nor allowed practice and is therefore censured by this meeting.' [8]

This statement, which was out of step with the prominent view in British society, probably developed over time from a minute from the Philadelphia Yearly Meeting that originated in 1688 in the Germantown Quaker Meeting. That year, a small group of German and Dutch settlers developed a 'Petition Against Slavery.' This group was accepted as part of the local Quaker Meeting but did not have the same view of enslavement as the English Quakers who regarded enslaved people as commodities necessary for economic development.

The petition, based on Matthew Chapter 7 verse 12

'Therefore, all things whatsoever ye would that men should do to you, do ye even so to them: for this is the law and the prophets.'

urged the Germantown Quaker Meeting to abolish slavery. It argued that every human, regardless of belief, colour, or ethnicity, had rights that should not be violated. The document asked readers to put themselves in the position of slaves and to take the ethics of equality seriously. Francis Daniel Pastorius and three other Quakers signed it on behalf of the Germantown Meeting.

This was the first protest against the enslavement of Africans made by a religious body in America and is now regarded as one of the first written public declarations of universal human rights.

Germantown Friends forwarded the petition to their monthly, quarterly, and yearly meetings without either approving or rejecting it. It was said to be 'too weighty a matter to be discerned.' The Philadelphia Yearly Meeting minuted that they would send the petition to the London Yearly Meeting without passing judgement on it. No reference to it appears in the London Yearly Minutes but it must have been a topic of conversation between Friends and have provoked a questioning of the practice of enslaving people resulting in the **1727** minute.

It was **1757** before any further comment was made on the enslavement of Africans. At the June 'Sufferings Meeting' in **1757**, at which William Dillworth of Lancaster Monthly and Preparative Meetings was present, the following minute was made:

'This meeting being apprehensive that some under our name both in this Nation and in the Colonies abroad are concerned for … in dealing with Negros. This Meeting for Sufferings is desired to send copys (sic) of several minutes of this meeting relating thereto, and also extracts of such advice from a printed Epistle on that subject, to the several counties of this Nation and Colonies abroad for their admonition and also to give them other advice as may appear to them necessary.' [9]

On the 15th of July 1757, a subcommittee of seven Friends reported to Meeting for Sufferings that after very careful examination, there appeared to be only one past Yearly Meeting minute concerning the slave trade and that had been issued thirty years previously and had merely censured the trade. The Meeting for Sufferings referred the matter back to London Yearly Meeting for further consideration.

In **1758**, London Yearly Meeting minuted that 'Friends should avoid reaping unrighteous profits from the iniquitous practice of dealing in negroes or other slaves.' [10]
The Epistle in **1758** stated that the slave trade was:

'a most unnatural traffic, whereby great numbers of mankind, free by nature are subjected to inextricable bondage…' [11]

In **1761**, London Yearly Meeting recommended that any Quakers found continuing in the slave trade should be disowned by their religious community. This was in response to a suggestion from the Philadelphia Meeting for Sufferings. The Epistle sent to the Pennsylvania Yearly Meeting by the London Yearly Meeting that year confirms this. It states that particular notice had been taken of their request and that a Minute of Disownment had, as a result, been adopted. [12]

That year, the Yearly Meeting also agreed that Query 12 should stand:

'Do you bear faithfully testing against bearing arms, for paying Trophy Money or being in any manner concerned in the Militia, in Privateering, letters of Marque, or in dealing in Prize Goods as such.' [13]

A Letter of Marque was a commission authorising privately owned ships (known as privateers) to capture enemy merchant ships during the war with France. Prize Goods captured from enemy merchant ships could include enslaved people.

limited to profit and loss, deaths of the enslaved and acquisitions? How much was spent on accommodation for the enslaved?

In contrast, Josia Booker, the manager, wrote to George Pickard:

'The people on this property are comfortably supplied with food and clothing by their respectable owners (John Bond and Quaker Abraham Rawlinson - son of Thomas Rawlinson, are named in the footnote as their owners) after the apportioned work of the day is over, it frequently occurs that the industrious have spare time to cultivate their plots of ground, the products of which, if not given their stock of poultry and pigs, is disposed of for articles of luxury, either in food or clothing. As an encouragement, we prepare the land for them by ploughing and harrowing.' [17]

The Booker family continued to be employed by the descendants of the Bond family. They themselves became plantation owners and founded the Booker shipping line out of Liverpool. The Booker Prize and Bookers Wholesale are household names linked in the 21st century to this family.

Lancaster ceased as an enslaving port when, in 1799, the Slave Trade Act decreed that slaving ships could only sail from Liverpool, London and Bristol. Some Lancaster merchants, including some of the Quaker merchants, moved their business to Liverpool till 1807 when the Abolition of the Slave Trade Act outlawed the British Atlantic Slave Trade. Some, however, retained their ownership of plantations till 1833 and beyond.

ABOLITION

1787 On the 22nd of May at No2 George Yard London (a printing shop), a group of 8 Quakers and 3 Anglicans met to establish 'The Society for Effecting the Abolition of the Slave Trade.'

1788 The Abolition of the Slave Trade was first taken before Parliament when 35 petitions were laid on the table of the House of Commons.

1790 On the 24th of December, the Quaker Meeting for Sufferings was concerned that Abolition was to go before Parliament in the new year. They asked Friends to apply to their Members of Parliament during the recess 'to require their furious attention to this weighty subject, and to endeavour to impress their minds with a just abhorrence of a practice repugnant to Humanity and Religion'. John Ady - Clerk.

This minute was sent to William Jepson and John Field of Lancaster Monthly Meeting. [18] There is no record in the archive of contact with the MPs for Lancaster, John Blackburne and John Dent.

1793 London Yearly Meeting minuted concern that abolition was taking so long and asked Friends to be steadfast in pursuing it.

1807 Parliament passed the Abolition of the Slave Trade Act outlawing the British Atlantic Slave Trade.

1833, Parliament passed the Abolition of Slavery Act ordering a gradual abolition of slavery in all British colonies.

British plantation owners received £20 million in compensation for their loss of the labour of the enslaved (equivalent to almost 2.2 billion in 2024). That money fed back into the British economy in many cases, fuelling the building of the railway companies and providing patronage to the arts and inventions. It took until 2015 for British tax payers to complete repayment of the loan raised to pay this compensation. Thus, any descendants of the enslaved, such as the Windrush generation, working and paying taxes in Britain were contributing to repaying this loan.

Those enslaved were not compensated and their freedom was bitter sweet. The Act established an apprenticeship scheme under which the emancipated continued to labour as indentured apprentices for their former owners for six years. Their lives did not change. At the end of their apprenticeship, they were cast out of most plantations without a job, money or place to live. They were replaced by indentured labour from elsewhere in the British Empire. This treatment of the enslaved has resulted in, for example, 'one-third of Jamaicans in 2024 waking up as squatters.' [19]

The abolition of the Transatlantic Chattel Slave Trade in 1803 further changed the African nations, leading to a collapse of their economies and making them ripe for colonisation. The whole continent was impacted and continues to be so with the plundering of resources long after colonialisation has ended. This has resulted in the nation-states in Africa being financially unable to combat the effects of climate change of which they bear the brunt. The loss and damage they now experience have their roots in the 18th-century enslaving industry in which some Lancaster Quakers participated.

The wounds created by the enslaving industry have not healed, leaving a legacy of trauma found today not just in the Caribbean, South America, and the United States of America but also in the black communities in Britain and the African nations from which the enslaved were taken.

LANCASTER PREPARATIVE MEETING AND THE ANTI-SLAVERY MOVEMENT

Lancaster's Quakers played a part in the anti-slavery movement but it was not until the British Atlantic Slave Trade had been abolished.

An **1821** letter from the Quaker abolitionist George Stacey, in the Meeting's archive, reveals that Quakers in Lancaster and Preston collected 16 pounds and 15 shillings for the Fund for Promoting the Total Abolition of the Slave Trade. This amount would have been the equivalent of £1,579 in November 2024, according to the Bank of England's Historic Inflation Rate Calculator.

Lancaster Friends who subscribed included John Dilworth £1, Bridget & Mary Walley £1, William Barrow £1, and William Satterthwaite 10sh.06d, George Barrow 10sh.06d, Lawson Walley 10sh.06d, William Birkett 10sh.06d, Samuel Satterthwaite 10sh.06d. (£1 in 1821 would be the equivalent to £93 in November 2024) Some of these Friends we will see were descendants of the Lancaster Quakers identified in this study as directly involved in trading enslaved people.

Lancaster and Preston Quakers had donated 'under the hope of our suitable aid being beneficial in abolishing the Slave Trade, which appears to have been continued by some nations with its usual horrors and sad consequences.' [20]

It was not until April **1845** that Lancaster Quakers decided to form their own Anti-Slavery Society in order to circulate anti-slavery texts and to express their unified solidarity with American Quakers who had been imprisoned while fighting for the freedom of the enslaved.

REFERENCES

1. Translation from Davenport, Frances Gardiner. Ed. *European Treaties bearing on the History of the United States and its Dependencies to 1648.* Carnegie Institution of Washington, Washington, D.C.: 1917, p. 23.
2. James Walvin – 'A World Transformed - Slavery in the Americas and the origins of global power.' 2022 Chapter 2.
3. Olivette Otele Professor of the Legacies and Memory of Slavery at SOAS University of London 2023. More than Money – The logic of slavery reparations _ The Guardian the 31st of March 2023.
4. Prof. William Pettigrew Lancaster University History Department - Register of British Slave Traders 2023
5. 'A World Transformed – Slavery in the Americas and the origin of Global Power' James Walvin 2022 page 74.
6. Katherine Gebner – 'Slavery in the Quaker World' 2019.
7. Testimony of Inequality – Chapter 2 by Elizabeth Cazden in Quakerism in the Atlantic World 1690 – 1830
8. Quaker Faith & Practice fifth edition 23.24
9. Lancaster Central & North Area Meeting Archive FRL21/1/1/31 - Minutes regarding ... and Friends involvement in slave trade 1757
10. **Appendix 1** - Book of Christian discipline of the Religious Society of Friends in Great Britain. Consisting of extracts on doctrine, practice and church government. Epistles, and other documents issued under sanction of the Yearly Meeting held in London from the first institution in 1672 to the year 1883. Extract from Chapter X
11. Yearly Meeting Printed Epistles 1758 Vol 1 page 308
12. Friends House MSS – Epistles Sent Vol 4 London Yearly Meeting to Pennsylvania Yearly Meeting May 1761
13. Lancaster Central & North Area Quaker Meeting Archive FRL 21/1/1/36 Minutes regarding the slave trade, elders, Yearly Meeting Epistles, attachment of Friends to their Monthly Meetings, encouragement of schools, peace query and state of society especially concerning pacifism as revealed by answers to queries, 1761.
14. Lancaster Central & North Area Quaker Meeting Archive FRL 21/1/1/56 Minutes regarding ... Friends' involvement with slave trade..., 1784
15. Lancaster Central & North Area Quaker Meeting Archive FRL 21/1/1/57 Minutes regarding Friends' involvement in slave trade ... 1785
16. George Pinckard MD: Notes on the West Indies, Written During the 1796 Expedition under the command of General Sir Ralph Abercromby. (Vol 2 pages 66-6)
17. Black Lives Matter and Legacies of Slave Ownership in Lancaster: The Bond's and the Booker Brothers in Guyan - Imogen Tyler 2020
18. Lancaster Central & North Area Quaker Meeting Archive FRL 21/2/4/4
19. Rev Gordon Cowans Retired Moderator of the United Church in Jamaica & Cayman Islands Churches Reparation Action Forum (CRAF) at the European Ecumenical Roundtable on the legacies of Slavery, Colonialism and Racism the 25th of May 2023.
20. Lancaster Central & North Area Quaker Meeting Archive FRL 1/1/1/1 Minute Book page 6.

LANCASTER QUAKER MERCHANTS IN THE 17TH & 18TH CENTURIES

It is important to note that university education was not available to Quakers in this period and very few opportunities were available to practice in the professions. Many early Quakers were in trade. They worked as artisans or worked the land as yeomen, tenant farmers or agricultural labourers. Under the 1661 Corporation Act, Quakers were also barred from civic life in cities established under a charter. Lancaster had been granted its first charter on the 12th of June, 1193. Thus, it is not surprising to find that Quakers in Lancaster and the surrounding district in the 17th & 18th centuries made their living from the land or trade. A number were moving from working the land to becoming merchants in the city. They required capital to hire and equip their premises. Many, including Lancaster Quakers William Stout and John Heathcote, started life as apprentices to Quaker merchants. Quaker Quarterly Meetings loaned money to help Friends set up in trade. George Fox had asked Friends to leave money in their Wills to provide support to others to set up a trade. Quaker merchants provided credit to each other by not requiring immediate payment for goods and services thus easing the way for many into the world of becoming a merchant.

Early Quakers throughout Britain operated an apprenticeship scheme for the young men in their families. Quaker Meetings made the actual arrangements and, in many cases, put up the considerable fees. This ensured that young men continued to be educated in 'the truth' as they entered work. Lancaster Monthly Meeting operated as a clearing house for masters seeking apprentices and apprentices seeking masters. The Monthly Meeting Minute Books record all these agreements. This extract, taken from the Minutes of the meeting held on the 6th day of the 8th month of 1759, provides two different examples:

'Friends of Wyersdale offer James Dillworth the sone (sic) of James Dillworth as a boy wanting a Master, and James Prodkter [sic] inclining to take an apprentice to the trade of a Hatter. Tho. Kendal and William Dillworth are desired to treat with him on that act, to report his proposals to next Mo. Meeting.'

'Friends of Yealand Meeting also offer to this Meeting Joseph the son of Thom. Adlington is a boy who wants a master and is informed his Father is inclined to take him apprentice for the term of seven years to his business as a Woolcomber & Worsted weaver, which is aggregable to this Meeting. It's agreed to allow him Six pounds as a fee. Forty Shillings to be paid on signing the Indenture. Forty shillings more at the end of year one and the residue at the end of the second year. It is left in the care of the Friends of Yealand to get the same perfected and report.' [1]

The Lancashire Quarterly Meeting Query 9 of that time made clear the way in which apprenticeships should be dealt with:

'Do any offers for Masters or Apprentices? Are they in their apprenticeships duly instructed and kept in good order? And are none put to apprenticeships to any but Friends? Do any Friends want Servants or Servants places?' [2]

Being 'outsiders' meant that Friends in the 17 & 18th centuries were bonded by a nation-wide network of 'mutual support that resulted in business linkages, capital flows and marriages.' [3] This was established through the way the Quaker movement was organised and by its strict codes of behaviour. We will see this played out in the family histories which follow.

To trade in Lancaster, early Quaker Merchants had first to become freemen or, as a non-freeman, pay an annual fine to be entered on the 'stallenge roll.' Both gave people the right to trade in Lancaster but each required the swearing of an oath. In 1693 Lancaster Monthly Meeting had agreed that Friends would stand by the form of words laid down by Christ instead of an oath,' that 'yea', 'yea' and 'nay', 'nay' ought to be stood and nothing more offered'. So, Lancaster Quakers were barred from trading as they did not swear oaths. Even when the Affirmations Act of 1695 became law, it was unacceptable to Lancaster Quakers as it contained the words 'in the presence of God'.

If you were not willing to swear or affirm you could not become a freeman. Early Lancaster Quakers would not have been able to prove Wills, enter answers in court, inherit copyholds or trade. However, in 1728, William Stout and two other Quakers did affirm a declaration for a stallenge to enable them to trade. [4] Many appear in Burgess Rolls and held positions of responsibility in the community, so there must have been some complicity to avoid the swearing of oaths or affirming declarations, possibly by allowing a Jurat (a statement) to be entered.

Entering the business world of the 17 & 18th centuries would have tested Quaker discipline. Quakers were warned 'not to run into debt beyond that which they were able to pay.' They were to 'be careful not to be concerned in the defrauding of the King of his customs and excise' and were to avoid 'making or selling of striped or figured stuff or other cloth for apparel.' Not all Lancaster Quaker Merchants and their families managed to live up to these requirements.

Business was unregulated and involved the taking of risks which could go very wrong. For example, in 1790, the London Gazette lists Lancaster Quaker Merchants Thomas Satterthwaite, Abraham Rawlinson, Thomas Hutton Rawlinson, Moss Lawson and Abraham Rawlinson & Co. amongst the creditors of the bankrupt Sir Francis Mannock deceased. [5]

Being in business involving the sea was a particularly risky occupation. Merchant ships engaged in the colonial trade could be embroiled in war captured by privateers or founder. The latter two happened on the same voyage to the ship *Employment,* owned by Lancaster Quakers Robert Lawson, Joshua Lawson, William Stout, George Godsalve, plus four non-Quakers on the return voyage from Barbados in 1702. It was captured as a prize by a French ship. The captain was taken hostage for a ransom and the First Mate was required to sail the ship back only for it to founder off Fleetwood. The crew and cargo were saved but the ship broke up. [6]

To marry, Quaker men had to make sure they had sufficient income to support a wife and family as there was no welfare to fall back on save that of the Quaker Meeting. The women Overseers were responsible for checking this prior to permission to marry. As a result, many did not marry until in their 30s or later and so for young Quaker men there was a real imperative to make money.

Quakerism was founded in an era emerging from centuries of unrest, including the civil war, which ended in 1651 and in which brutal and gross torture was rampant. It was a time when Lancaster was known as the 'Hanging Town' because so many were condemned to death in the court at the castle. It was a society so different from ours in the 21st century that it is difficult to comprehend. The city and villages around Lancaster were small until the money from the enslaving industry was spent by the wealthy merchants on building homes, public buildings and warehouses.

It was the early trading connections of John Lawson and John Hodgson with Virginia and Barbados and the building of John Lawson's Sugar House on St Leonard's Steet that led to the start of a change in fortune for the city and the involvement of so many Lancaster Merchants in trade with the West Indies and America.

The history of the Lancaster Quaker community is linked with the earliest phase of the development of Quakerism. George Fox visited Lancaster in 1652 and wrote in his journal:

'In the afternoon, I went to the steeplehouse at Lancaster and declared the truth both to the priest and people, laying open before them the deceits they live in and directing them to the power of the spirit of God, which they wanted. But they haled me out and stoned me along the street till I came to John Lawson's house.'

In1952, during cleaning operations in the basement of Towneley Hall, Burnley, there were discovered several crumpled sheets of paper, which were found to be large-scale town plans of Lancaster and Preston in 1684 and other areas of Lancashire. The map gives a clear idea of the scale of Lancaster in 1684. [7] Many of the buildings in Market Street on the map are thought to be temporary wooden structures as they were built to replace those burnt down in 1643 during the civil war. The Quaker Meeting House is shown on Kiln Lane.

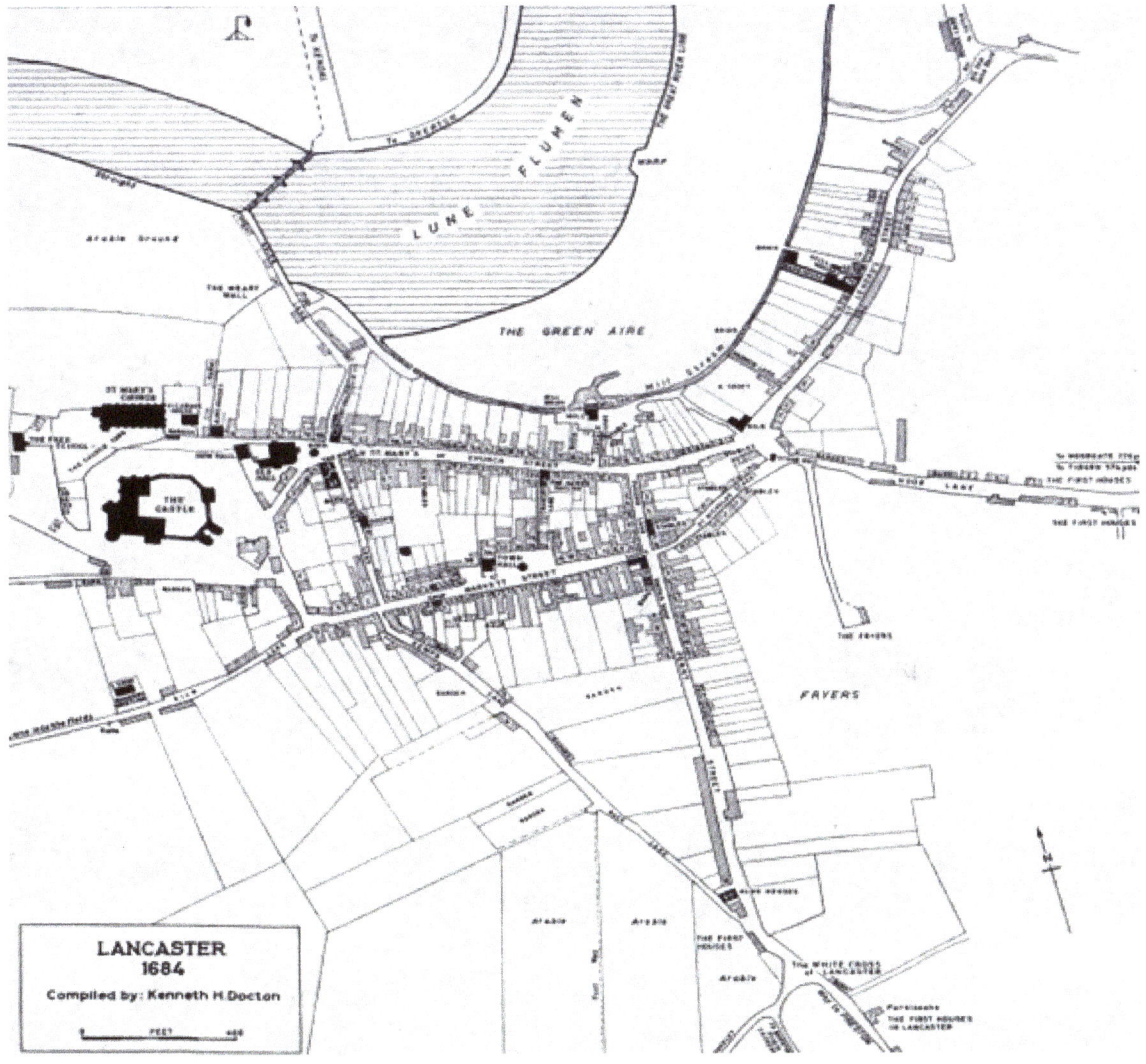

Map of Lancaster 1684 Kenneth H Docton

Most of the Quakers involved in the enslaving industry came to Lancaster from the surrounding area. The Rawlinsons and Satterthwaites are originally from Hawkshead, John Heathcote from Derbyshire and Dodshon Foster from Durham. The Dillworth family was more local. They came from Wyersdale in the Trough of Bowland. Only Robert Lawson, son of John, was born and bred in Lancaster.

Biographies of those Lancaster Quakers involved either directly in trafficking the enslaved or in owning plantations or importing and selling goods produced by the enslaved follow in the form of family histories giving detail, where possible, of their business actions and their involvement in Quaker Meetings.

I have chosen to use family histories to record this information. The study of them shows clearly how wealth accrued from the enslaving industry and passed down through generations was used to change not only their standard of living, their social standing, their children's education and marriage prospects, but also the local built environment of Lancaster and district and prime the industrial revolution in Britain. These family histories show how investments of capital from the enslaving industry supported the development of the industrial revolution. This inheritance process resulted in the monetary profit from the enslaving industry being normalised by the third or fourth generations.

REFERENCES

1. Lancaster Central & North Area Quaker Meeting Archive: FRL 2/1/1/1/2 Lancaster Monthly Meeting Minute Book.
2. LC&NAQM Archive: FRL 1/1/1/13 Quarterly Meeting Minute Book 1776 – 1805
3. Philanthropy from Aristotle to Zuckerberg. Paul Vallely – the 02nd of October 2020 article in the Friend.
4. The Social and Political Relations of the Lancaster Quaker Community 1688 – 1740 Nicholas Morgan in Early Lancaster Friends published by the Centre for North-West Regional Studies University of Lancaster 1978 page 23.
5. Find My Past – Newspapers and periodicals – London Gazette Issue: 13210.
6. Autobiography of William Stout of Lancaster Wholesale and Retail Grocer and Ironmonger page 62.
7. Lancaster 1684 Kenneth H. Docton, M.I.MUN.E.

THE LAWSON FAMILIES

Table 4.1

THE LAWSON FAMILIES

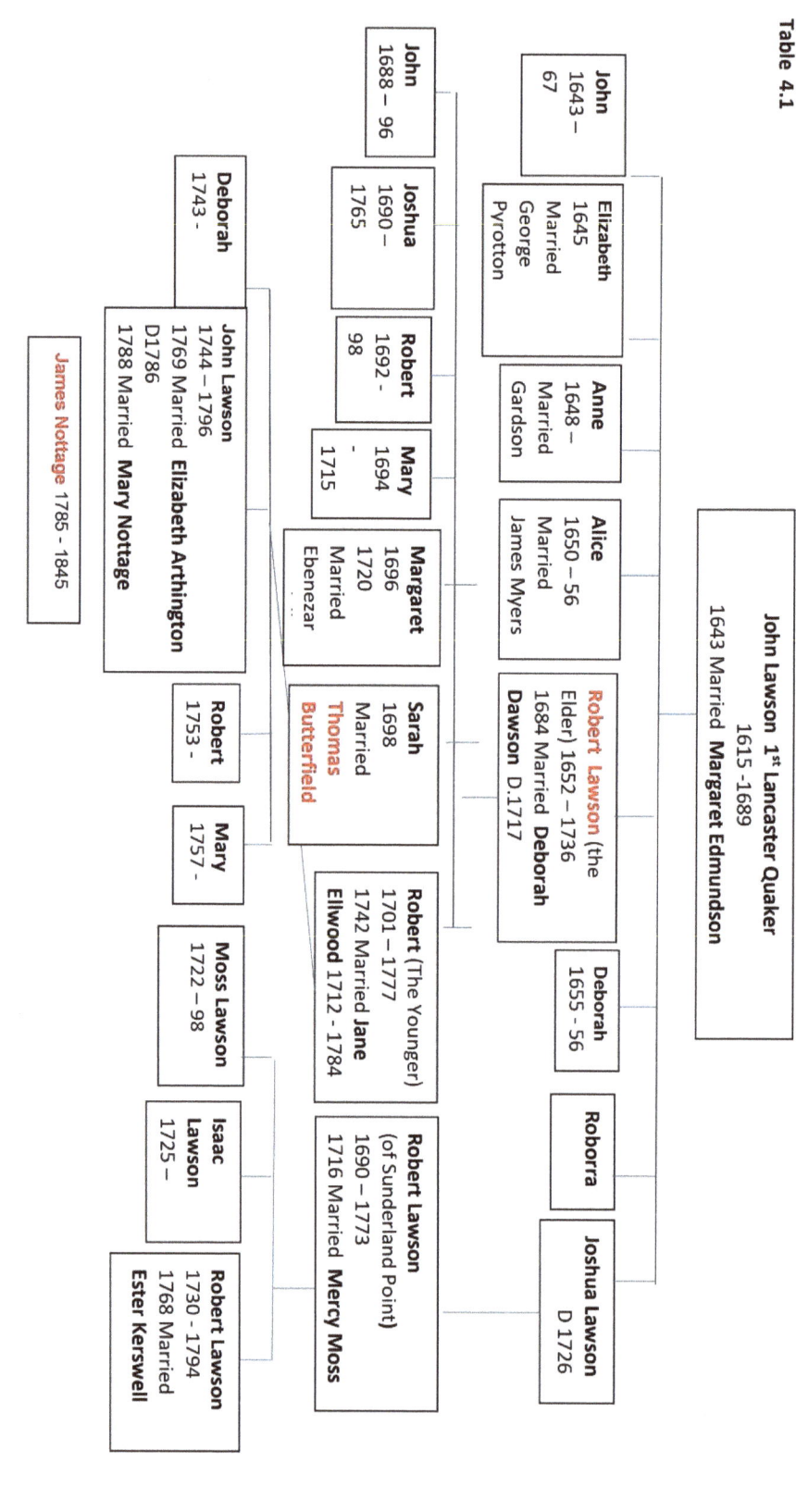

John Lawson 1615 – 1689

John Lawson of St Leonards Street Lancaster encountered George Fox in 1652 when he sheltered him from the crowd stoning him through the city from St Mary's Church. This event was to transform his life and that of his family.

In 1652, he was a well-established Lancaster merchant and sugar importer, a grocer. He had built and operated a Sugar House at 15 St Leonards St. Thus, in the mid-17th century, John had established links with sugar plantations in the West Indies, on which the enslaved worked, shipping sugar or molasses to his sugar house through his wharf on the river. Sugar was first exported from the Eastern Caribbean in 1641, and by 1650, Barbados was producing 7,000 tons of sugar, mainly produced by enslaved imported Africans.[1] John must have been involved from the very early stages of this trade. Sugar Houses either processed raw brown sugar (muscovado) into white sugar to be sold in the form of cones or loaves and/or distilled rum from the molasses, the by-product of the sugar refining process.

We know from Quaker William Stout's autobiography of this time that some sugar was exported from Lancaster. He says that 'not above one-fourth of the sugar imported to Lancaster was consumed in Lancaster.' He records that half of the sugar imported was exported in 1709 to Holland, Germany and the Northern Kingdoms. John Lawson and his descendants, with this early start in the trade, would have been involved in both importing and exporting.

The sweetness of sugar hid the violence of its production. Caribbean sugar plantations were infamous for their high rate of mortality and deficiencies in diet, shelter and clothing. The working conditions were brutal and tropical disease contributed to a death toll that was 50% higher on sugar plantations than on coffee plantations.

Following John's encounter with Fox in 1652, he became a follower and travelled preaching George Fox's words. He suffered much for speaking 'truth.'

In 1652, for preaching in the Steeple-house Yard (the churchyard) at Malpas, he was set in the stocks for four hours and imprisoned at the country goal at West Houghton for twenty-three weeks.
[2]

"Accusations against John Lawson, of Lancaster, by him answered" is the title of a tract printed for him in quarto in 1653 held by the British Museum. This pamphlet was almost not published but Margaret Fell of Swarthmoor Hall wrote to her husband, Judge Fell, urging him to have it published. Thus, John Lawson was among the 70 Quakers known as 'The First Publishers'.

1653, he travelled with Richard Hubberthorne from Yealand to Wales and Cheshire, spreading George Fox's words.

In 1654, for speaking in a steeple-house at Lancaster, he was fined £20 at the Assizes and, for non-payment, was imprisoned for a year in Lancaster Castle. (£20 in 1654 equates £4,358 in 2024).

During his imprisonment, he wrote three letters to Margaret Fell at Swarthmoor Hall.
Then, on the 20th of November in 1660, 'for meeting together,' he was taken to Lancaster Castle prison and committed for refusing the oath tendered to him in court.

Early Quakers (Friends of the Truth) in Lancaster could not by law meet to worship. It was the 1687 Declaration of Indulgence issued by James II that gave Friends the right to register and meet freely in their Meeting Houses. Thus, the building of the Lancaster Quaker Meeting House in 1677 was seen by the local magistrates as an act of defiance. Friends meeting there in the intervening 10 years were regularly taken from the First Day (Sunday) Meeting for Worship and imprisoned in the castle, men, women and children. The Quaker Quarterly Meeting paid for candles and fuel and Friends were appointed to take in food and blankets.

John was an important member of the city's commercial and political community. Still, in 1668, he was dismissed from the office of Bailiff of the Customs for refusing to take the oath as his Quaker principles directed.

In 1679, he erected a stone bridge, Merchant's Bridge, over the Mill Dam from his garden to the 'Green Area.' In 1680, he was 'permitted to erect a wharf adjacent his new bridge 20 yards long and freemen to have use of it on payment of 4d. a ton'. [3] John continued to be a significant merchant in the city.

The 1684 directory of Lancaster tells us that John traded at 15 &17 St Leonards Street, where he had the Sugar House, a Still and Warehouse. This indicates that John distilled rum from the molasses. It also confirms he had built a wharf on the river. In addition, he had a property at 9 Pudding Lane – now Cheapside. There is no evidence that he ever traded in enslaved people but in trading in sugar and molasses produced by the enslaved, he contributed to the enslaving industry.

John died in September 1689, aged 74. The grounds of the Meeting House at this stage were not used for burials. The Mooreside Burial Ground had been established in 1661 and he was accorded a Quaker burial there. His memorial stone is now in the porch of Lancaster Meeting House.

His Will was granted probate on the 7th of November 1689. John left his property and money to his children. John, his eldest son, had died in 1667, so Robert and Joshua were the two sons who inherited, with daughters Roborra and Anne Gardson, sons-in-law James Myers and George Pyrotton and grandchildren. [4]

What is clear from this biography is that trading with the West Indies in goods produced by the enslaved was well-established among Lancaster Merchants prior to the formation of the Religious Society of Friends in Lancaster.

Robert Lawson (the Elder) 1652 – 1735
Sons John 1688- 1769, Joshua 1690 – 1765 & Robert (the Younger) 1701- 1771

Robert Lawson (the Elder), son of John Lawson, was baptised on the 25th of April 1652 at St Mary's Church Lancaster, the same year in which his father became a Quaker. Robert was brought up as a Quaker and followed his father into his business considerably expanding it.

In 1679, there was a conveyance of land from Thomas Rawlinson to Robert, which may have been for additional land at the Meeting House for burials.

In 1684, Robert and Deborah Dawson took each other in marriage in Lancaster Meeting House. [5] They had eight children, of whom 2 died in childhood. In 1703 Robert was admitted as a Free Burgess of the city.

In 1708, he was appointed with William Stout to care for the pulling down of the original Meeting House as it was not large enough to hold the General Meeting of the four northern counties. It was to be 'built double the size costing £180.' [6] William, in his autobiography, does not provide us with any detail of how the £180 was raised. However, the Quaker Minute Book 1669 – the 05th of April 1711 shows that funding was by subscriptions from each Preparatory Meeting in the Lancaster Monthly Meeting. [7] In 1709, they raised £149. 0sh. 08d, (the equivalent of £22,597 in 2024.)

Robert invested in the South Sea Company experiencing substantial losses in 1721 when the South Sea Bubble burst. War with Spain, the seizing of company property, and corruption amongst the Board of Directors (including government cabinet members) all led to the stock collapsing in 1721. Nevertheless, this company trafficked 41,000 enslaved Africans during its existence. Robert avoided bankruptcy, having invested heavily in land in Lancashire.

Robert was also a part owner, with Augustine Greenwood, a Presbyterian Merchant and James Myers of Swarthmoor Quaker Meeting, of the colonial trading ship *Content* which had 6 cannons to protect it. Robert was not disowned for carrying 'instruments of war' on this ship, so breaking the Quaker Peace Testimony. He also had a 50% share in the ship *Robert*. [8]

Between 1729 and 1738, Robert, with his youngest son Robert, born 1701 (known as Robert the Younger), sent 5 vessels to Barbados. [9] In fact, Robert the Elder died in 1736, so it was his son, Robert (the Younger), trading in 1737/8. His two brothers, Joshua and John also had a ship, *Endeavour*. They exported a rich variety of goods. The *Sarah* trading with Barbados in 1737 shipped out beef, butter, sundry oats, felt hats, feathers, men's shoes, tallow candles, pewter, snuff, northern cotton, cordage, potatoes, cheese, nuts and grunts (probably ale) all to be sold to plantation owners. The ship brought back sugar, cotton, mahogany and tobacco amongst other goods purchased from them.

Robert's partner for two of these voyages to Barbados was Isaac Moss, a Quaker Hosier from Manchester. It is thought that this link gave the Lawsons access to Lancashire cotton goods for export. Robert's other partners included the Lancaster Quaker Miles Townson.

In 1733, Robert and Deborah's youngest daughter Sarah married Thomas Butterfield at St Mary's church Lancaster. For 'marrying out and not in the manner of Friends', Sarah was disowned by Lancaster Quaker Meeting. This marriage brought the Lawsons into a family relationship with an Anglican trafficking enslaved people and owning a plantation. Thomas Butterflied was one of the first Lancaster Merchants to enter the Transatlantic Chattel Slave Trade from Lancaster with his ship the *Expedition* in 1744. His brother William owned 7 Slave trading ships out of Lancaster. I have found no evidence of any mutual business advantage developing from this marriage.

It is said Robert the Younger withdrew from the colonial trade in the 18th century. Melinda Elder notes that 'the Lawson name is notably absent from the records relating to the Lancaster slave trade.' [10] Nonetheless, the Lawsons dealt in goods produced by the labour of the enslaved, further supported the plantations by trading goods to them, and Robert (the Elder) invested in a company that bought and sold significant numbers of Africans who had been enslaved prior to the Africa Trade starting from Lancaster. They certainly contributed to the enslaving industry.

Robert the Elder died in 1736 and was buried in the Quaker burial ground at Mooreside.

Robert's Will makes clear the extent of his investments in land using money gained from his trading with the West Indies. He left to his son John the land he owned in Caton and estates in York, Addingham and Halton. To Robert (the Younger), he left the Sugar House, barns, stables and shops, land in Scotforth, Stody, Heysham, Poulton, Brooks, Chipping, Claughton, Woodplumpton, Goosnargh and trading in York. He left money to his son Joshua. [11]

John 1688 – 1769 and Joshua 1690 – 1765

Robert's older sons, John and Joshua, both traded in the West Indies with the ship *Endeavour* between 1728 and 1738. [12] There is no further information about their trading activity, but these third-generation Quakers were undoubtedly benefiting from selling goods made by enslaved people and contributed to the enslaving industry.

They were both admitted as Fee Burgesses of Lancaster, John in 1715/16 and Joshua in 1722/23.

Robert Lawson (the Younger) 1701 – 1771

Robert the Younger became a Free Burgess of Lancaster in 1724/5. We have already seen that with his father, he had sent at least five ships to Barbados between 1729 and 1738.

In 1746 he also served as a common council man with Abraham Rawlinson, Thomas Hutton Rawlinson and Miles Birket, all being Quakers, and we will see the Rawlinsons had knowledge of and participated in enslaving Africans and owning them on plantations. In 1746, these Quakers would have been able to affirm rather than swear an oath to take up this role in the community.

In 1742, Robert and Jane Ellewood took each other in marriage. They had four children: Deborah 1743, John 1744, Robert 1753 and Mary 1757.

Robert, as a West Indian colonial trader trading out of Lancaster, must have been aware of the enslaving activities of other Lancaster Quaker Merchants. There is, however, no evidence that he was himself involved in trafficking or owning enslaved people. However, in trading in goods from the West Indies, he was contributing to the enslaving industry.

John Lawson 1744 – 1796

Robert (the Younger) and Jane's son John also became a colonial trader and may have expanded his activity in Barbados. He was admitted to the Burgess roll in 1761/2, classed as 'a gentleman son of Robert'. Thus, by 1761 money gained from trading with plantations enabled him to improve his social standing in the community. He also contributed to the enslaving industry.

John and Elizabeth Arthington took each other in marriage in 1769 at Brighouse, Yorkshire. They had six children of whom four, Robert 1773, John 1776, Mary 1778 and Jane 1780, survived to adulthood.

John may have been involved in privateering as he was visited by the Monthly Meeting in September 1779 along with Abraham and Thomas Rawlinson for taking a French ship by a letter of Marque – i.e. privateering. [13] He apologised to the Meeting in October 1779.

He was disowned on the 3rd of December 1781 for adultery, apparently the second time he had committed adultery! Again, he offered profuse apologies. [14]

Elizabeth died in 1786, and in 1788, John re-married in what Friends termed an 'irregular marriage'. He married Mary Nottage (a Lancaster Quaker widow and mother of James Barton Nottage) in Scarborough in a church, so he was married by a priest and not 'in the manner of Friends.' John's marriage appears to have been aided by his cousin Moss Lawson. The archive correspondence in 1789 between Lancaster and Grace Church Quaker Meeting reveals that both John and Moss had travelled to Scarborough together twice prior to the marriage and that John Rowntree had reported these facts to the Lancaster Meeting. John and Mary were disowned. [15] To be disowned twice is careless, but three times!

John died out of membership in 1796, as did his wife Mary Lawson in 1798. Both, however, were buried at the Moorside Quaker Burial Ground. He left his property and land to family and friends, including his cousin Moss Lawson, after making provision for his servants for their lifetime. [16]

His son 'Robert Lawson, son of John late of Lancaster,' was admitted as a Free Burgess in 1817/18. He is described as 'Esquire of Middleton Lodge in Richmond.' Here we see an example of how money derived from trading the enslaved and in goods produced by the enslaved passed down through the generations and enhanced the social standing of recipients. This Robert Lawson moved from being a merchant to a gentleman not needing to work.

Today, we do not disown Friends who are not in unity with us in the way that early Friends did. The Lancashire Central & North Area Quaker Meeting's archive contains many records of early Friends being disowned and readmitted after admitting 'their fault.'

Why was disownment used so much and why was it such a severe punishment? The young church was keen to maintain unity. A way of doing that was to ensure that Friends who fell short by getting into debt, marrying outside the society or joining a militia were visited, 'laboured with', in some cases supported, and in others disowned till they were willing to make an apology 'admitting their fault' to the meeting.

Most Friends who were disowned did apologise because the Quaker Meeting registered birth, marriages and deaths, thus saving them the fees they would have had to pay to the vicar. If a Friend did not apologise, the only way they could have children recognised would have been to join the Church of England and be baptised as an adult, incurring a cost. The Quaker Meeting also assisted families who, through no fault of their own, were in financial need. This would not have been available to those who were disowned. Thus, to be in membership provided a safety net in troubled times. In addition, because of the way in which Friends became known in their community as trustworthy and as speakers of the truth, membership gave them a good standing in their local community.

Footnote to John Lawson's biography

James Barton Nottage 1785 – 1845 John Lawson's step son

Some writing about James Nottage suggests he was a Quaker and owned enslaved people. James was indeed both but not at the same time. Born to Quaker parents in November 1785 in Birmingham, his father, James Nottage, died 2 years later. He was an only child.

That year, with his mother Mary (neé Barton), who was originally from York according to her marriage certificate, he came to Lancaster. There are Certificates of Transfer dated 1787 for them both in the archive. But we are not given information about why she moved to Lancaster.

In 1788, when James was just 3 years of age, Mary, as we have already seen, married John Lawson and was disowned. They appear to have continued to attend Meetings for Worship. Certainly James did, for James Barton Nottage was himself 'disowned' by the Monthly Meeting on the 26th of December 1803 when just 17/18 years old for 'voluntarily enlisting in a military organisation'. [17]

When Napoleon was threatening to invade Britain, a militia was established in many cities by the 1757 Militia Act. Men were chosen by ballot and expected to serve or pay a fine or find a substitute to serve. Many Lancaster Quakers were imprisoned for refusing to take either of these steps. [18] The Lancaster militia had been stood down in 1782 but was recalled in April 1803. That is when it appears that James was balloted and chose to join rather than be imprisoned or pay a fine.

It is highly unlikely that he was a Quaker Merchant at that time. Given his age, it is much more likely that he was setting himself up as a merchant or just coming out of an apprenticeship. It was not until 1806/7 that he was admitted to the Lancaster Burgess Rolls as a Merchant. [19]

During his life time he did not 'admit his fault' and so was not readmitted into membership. When he became a Merchant, he was no longer a Quaker, nor was he when he owned plantations and was compensated for the enslaved people he owned.

He married Jane Alston in 1807 at St Mary's Church (The Priory), and their 3 children were baptised there. One, also James Barton Nottage, became a surgeon in Liverpool, pre-deceasing his father in 1842.

James was in partnership with George Burrow, a resident of St Leonard's Gate. George Burrow served as the city's mayor on three separate occasions: 1828, 1833 and 1835/6. He was prominent in the city in the industrial sector, having inherited the White Cross cotton mill in 1827. He owned the mill with his business partner, Thomas Housman Higgin. George and James had an office on Market Street for the merchant business of Burrow and Nottage.

James Barton Nottage owned five estates/plantations, one in the Bahamas and four in the Virgin Islands. In 1836, he was compensated for the ownership of 360 enslaved people. He received a total of £5,738.14s.3d, (£550,677 in 2024). [20]

James died in March 1845 and was buried at Lancaster St Mary's Church (The Priory) their burial record states he was 'CofE'.

Robert Lawson of Sunderland 1692 - 1773
Son of Joshua Lawson & Grandson of John Lawson, founder of Lancaster Preparative Meeting

Robert and Mercy Moss (daughter of hosier Isaac Moss) took each other in marriage on the 10th of May 1716 at Hardshaw Monthly Meeting Manchester. [21]

Robert developed the port of Sunderland Point Dock as an outpost of the Port of Lancaster from 1720-1723. It is claimed that the first bail of cotton for the Lancashire cotton industry was landed there. Thus we find Robert not only trading in goods produced from the labour of enslaved people but also operating a port to enable that trade to develop in Lancaster so clearly supporting and oiling the wheels of the wider enslaving industry.

Stonework from the ruined Cockersand Abbey just across the river may have been used in the construction of the quay and buildings. The buildings included two large warehouses, an anchor smithy, a block maker's shop and a rope walk. This meant that all the equipment necessary for the building or repairing and fitting out of ships could take place at Sunderland Point. Lancaster Merchants expecting their ships from the West Indies or America would gather in the room of Sunderland Hall, built in 1683, facing the sea to await their arrival.

Initially this was a bustling port. Ships could unload here or wait for the tide before moving up to the main dock at St. Georges Quay in Lancaster and registering at the Customs House. In time, as Glasson Dock was fully developed, Sunderland Point as a port became redundant. [22]

Robert was declared bankrupt in 1728 but does not seem to have been disowned by Friends despite Quakers being entreated not to 'run into debt beyond what they were able to pay'. William Stout provides us with a graphic description that gives an entirely different account to those who suggest the bankruptcy was because of the start of the development of nearby Glasson Dock.

'In the 4th month of this year, Robert Lawson of Sunderland Point failed in his credit, who had done as much in merchandise here as all the rest and had good success in trade but employed the profit in superfluity of buying land at great prices, and building chargeable and unnecessary houses, barns, gardens, and other fancies, and costly furniture, so that he overshot himself and a commission of bankrupt got out against him, and as he took up great sums from the collectors of the customs, land tax &c, the same was first paid. His debts were about £14,000 (having a value in 2024 of £2,120,917), of which about 14s in the pound was paid, but it was supposed he had so much as would have paid it all. If it could have been done without charges, and that if he had not been so extravagant in purchasing buildings and other superfluities, he might be worth £3,000 or £4,000.' [23]

There is a grave at Sunderland Point of an enslaved young man who died in a barn there in 1736. The story is that he was unwell, so he was left by his master, who went to Lancaster on business. Ironically, the eulogy on the grave was written by Rev. James Watson, whose brother William Watson was a prolific Lancaster enslaver and who we will see married into the Quaker-enslaving Satterthwaite family.

Robert died in 1773 at Sunderland Point and was buried in Lancaster.

Robert and Mercy had eight children, of whom 4 survived. Their sons Moss Lawson, Isaac Lawson and Robert Lawson eventually moved away from Lancaster.

Moss Lawson became a merchant and a colonial trader. In 1746/7, he was admitted as a free Burgess of Lancaster. [24] On the 15th of June 1790 he is listed in the London Gazette as a creditor of Sir Francis Mannock along with other Lancaster Quaker Merchants. He died in Gainsborough in 1798.

Isaac Lawson became a mariner and a sea captain, making his home in Bristol and marrying Mary Tiler, a non-Quaker, in 1753. His two children, however, were registered in the documents of the Bristol Quaker Meeting: Robert 1754 and Elizabeth 1756, both born in their home in Castle Green, close to the house of his brother Robert. Was Isaac involved in the Bristol slave trade or just the colonial trade? For whom did he sail ships?

Robert Lawson also settled in Bristol, establishing a glass bottle manufacturing company, Lawson & Co, with other Quakers, Fry & Frampton. Their company was part of a large glass manufacturing industry in Br0istol. In 1767/8, Robert was admitted as a Free Burgess of Lancaster – 'of Bristol, glass maker'[25]. In 1768, Robert Lawson of Lancaster and Ester Kerswell took each other in marriage in Bristol Meeting House. The marriage certificate makes clear that this is Robert Lawson, son of Robert Lawson of Sunderland Point.

In 1790, Lawson and Co twice sent goods to Charleston, America:
- On the 08th of April 1790, on the *Westbury,* 14,000 empty glass bottles.

- On the 14th of June 1790, on the *Elizabeth,* 4,548 empty glass bottles. [26]

There is no evidence of Robert being involved in the Bristol Slave Trade but he would have been aware of the Bristol Quakers who were enslaving whose number included John Fry. In trading with Charleston, he was contributing to the enslaving industry.

REFERENCES

1. A World Transformed - Slavery in the Americas and the Origins of Global Power - James Walvin 2022 - Robinson - page 43
2. Sufferings of Friends 1653 – 1700 - Joseph Besse 1767
3. Lancaster 1684 - Kenneth H Docton
4. Lancashire Archives R57B/8 Lancashire Archives Probate Index Archdeaconry of Richmond (1533-1748)
5. Find My Past website - Marriage and birth records.
6. Autobiography of William Stout, of Lancaster Wholesale and Retail Groser and Ironmonger – Forgotten Books - page 76
7. Lancaster Central & North Area Quaker Meeting Archive Minute Book - FRL 1/1/1/1
8. N Morgan: The Social and Political Relations of the Lancaster Quaker Community 1688 – 1740 in Early Lancaster Friends - pages 24 & 25
9. The Slave Trade and Economic Development of Eighteenth-Century Lancaster. M. Elder 1992 - Ryburn Academic - Pages 25/6.
10. The Slave Trade and Economic Development of Eighteenth-Century Lancaster. M. Elder 1992 - Ryburn Academic - Page 116
11. Robert Lawson (the Elder's) Will Lancashire Archive R58B/5
12. The Slave Trade and Economic Development of Eighteenth-Century Lancaster. M. Elder 1992 - Ryburn Academic - Pages 25/6.
13. LC&NAQM Archive – Disownments - FRL2/1/5/73
14. LC&NAQM Archive – Disownments - FRL2/1/5/76
15. *LC&NAQM Archive FRL2/1/33/44 Correspondence concerning Mary Nottage and John Lawson's irregular marriage and Moss Lawson's role in it -11 Nov 1788 - the 14th of October 1789 -10 items*
16. John Lawson's Will Lancashire Archive R1176/38
17. LC&NAQM Archive FRL/2/1/1/16 Monthly Meeting Minute Book the 06th of February 1797 - the 02nd of March 1807
18. LC&NAQM Archive FRL 2/1/33/22 Lawyer's answer to questions on imprisonment of Friends under the Militia Act, for not paying for substitutes n.d. [c.1750].
19. The Rolls of the Freemen of the Borough of Lancaster. 1688 to 1840.- page 235
20. University College London Legacies of British Slavery Database www.ucl.ac.uk/lbs/
21. www.findmypast/marriages England & Wales, Society of Friends (Quaker) 1578 – 1841
22. www.sunderlandpoint.net
23. Autobiography of William Stout, of Lancaster Wholesale and Retail Groser and Ironmonger – Forgotten Books - page 114
24. The Rolls of the Freemen of the Borough of Lancaster 1688 to 1840. Vol 087 page 195
25. The Rolls of the Freemen of the Borough of Lancaster 1688 to 1840. Vol 087 page 209
26. Trade of Bristol in the 18th century – Bristol Record Society Publication Vol XX

YOUNG MEN WHO CAME TO LANCASTER TO MAKE THEIR FORTUNES

John Heathcote 1730 – 1758

John, born to Cornelius, the second son of an aristocratic Quaker family in Derbyshire, was apprenticed to Lancaster Quaker Thomas Satterthwaite in 1748 for a premium of £100, (£18,428 in 2024). [1] His Grandfather, Sir John Heathcote (1670 – 1743), was the first Quaker in the family. It is said he corresponded with William Penn, founder of Pennsylvania.[2]

John's relatives, John Heathcote and Sir Gilbert Heathcote were both investors in an enslaving ship, *Marlborough,* which sailed out of London in 1702 and 1703 to the Gold Coast and trafficked 548 enslaved Africans to Jamaica. So it is probably not surprising that John was apprenticed in Lancaster to a Quaker known to be involved in the enslaving industry. As Thomas' apprentice he met the many Lancaster traders in enslaved people, particularly the Quakers. Once John's apprenticeship was concluded he set up his own company. He is said to have entered the 'Africa Slave Trade' in 1752 when just 22 years of age. [3] That year he also became a Free Burgess. [4]

In 1753, he and Millicent Satterthwaite, Thomas' sister, married at St Mary's Church. Lancaster Meeting records show that John and Millicent were disowned by Friends that year. Their daughter Mary was born on 27 May 1753 and is registered in the Quaker records. Mary was clearly conceived prior to their marriage. They had chosen to be married by a priest and not 'after the manner of Friends' as their subsequent Acknowledgement of Fault to Lancaster Meeting makes clear.

'It hath been a matter of no small concern and affliction to ourselves that by our imprudence in joining ourselves together in marriage in a manner contrary to the wholesome rules established amongst Friends …' [5]

They probably did this rather than face the Lancaster Quaker Women Overseers whose permission they would have needed to take each other in marriage in the Quaker Meeting.

They went on to have three more children, all also registered in the Quaker records: Cornelius 1754, whose story follows, Elizabeth 1755 and John 1758.

John partnered with Dodshon Foster who he met at Lancaster Quaker Meeting. Together with Richard Millerson, a Sea Captain, they owned the *Barlborough,* a 40-ton enslaving ship built and registered in Lancaster. The *Barlborough was* named after the Heathcote family estate in Derbyshire. The Voyages Database records that the ship had 6 guns. Lancaster Meeting was clearly turning a blind eye to the use of these 'instruments of war' on the *Barlborough* as there is no record in the minute books of John and Dodshon being challenged for this installation which was clearly against the Quaker Peace Testimony and arises from George Fox's words:

'I told [The Commonwealth Commissioners] I lived in the virtue of that life and power that took away the occasion of all wars…I told them I was come into the covenant of peace which was before wars and strife were.' 24.01 Quaker Faith and Practice.

The *Barlborough* set out from Lancaster in 1753 for the Guinea Coast with a crew of 14, presumably local Lancaster men. They acquired 118 enslaved people and transported them to Kingston, Jamaica for sale. Only 101 disembarked. [6]

From this voyage, the ship brought back to Lancaster 62 hogsheads and tierces (casks) of sugar; 5 tons of Fustick (an American tree of the mulberry family *Maclura tinctoria* from which yellow dye is extracted); 40 bags of ginger; 40 tons of mahogany and 23 bags of cotton. These goods were either sold on in Lancaster, the mahogany probably to the burgeoning Gillow furniture business, or in the case of cotton sent onward for sale in Manchester where the cotton industry was becoming established.

Further enslaved people trafficking voyages were made in 1754 and 1756. In 1754, of the 164 enslaved who embarked, 24 died on the voyage and in 1756, of the 168 who embarked, only 144 disembarked. All the surviving enslaved were sold in Kingston Jamacia. [6] Thus, on these three voyages, 450 enslaved embarked, of whom 385 were sold, but 65 perished at sea.

In 1756, John's enslaving ship *Bold,* which carried 150 enslaved people, owned by Heathcote and Company and in which Dodshon Foster had shares, put into Bridgetown, Barbados. [7] At the time of writing this ship is not recorded on the Voyages Database. The *Bold* was a 70-ton ship. Its return carried a cargo of 64 hogsheads & 19 tierces of sugar, 11 puncheons of rum, 7 tons of logwood & 14 bags of cotton.

John was also in business with William Watson, the son of the Anglican vicar of Crosby Ravensworth in Cumbria. Together with Miles Barber in 1758, they owned the *Cato,* also an Africa enslaving ship. [8] This was the largest enslaving ship to sail from Lancaster. In 1758, the *Cato* carried 400 enslaved and in 1761 it carried 672 enslaved to Barbados. This increase led to conditions in which 112 died.

John died on 28th March 1758 aged just 28. He was buried at Woodhouse, Balby Monthly Meeting, Yorkshire. It is not possible to determine why he was there or how he died. [9] He left Millicent with four small children to care for, one born just 20 days prior to his death. In his short life, John had been a prolific trafficker of enslaved people.

In 1761, Millicent married William Watson, John's trafficking partner, at The Priory Church of St Mary Lancaster. Millicent was again disowned, this time for 'marrying out.' She appears to have not only married a man 'not of Friends persuasion' and been married by a Priest but also to have been baptised, described by Friends as 'sprinkled' in this minute.

'In answer to the Queries. Friends of Lancaster inform this that Millicent Heathcote, widow of John Heathcote late of their Meeting, hath joined herself in Marriage with a young man not of our Religious persuasion by a Priest contrary to the advice of Friends who laboured with her on occasion and the established rules of their Society; She was having also previously submitted to be sprinkled & afterwards publically resorted to the places of worship amongst the Church of England so called, by which her disorderly conduct hath forfeited her Unity with Friends until by sincere repentance manifested by a suitable conduct and acknowledgement she give satisfaction to this Meeting; nothing further offered on the said Queries are continued under Friends care.' [10]

Millicent did not return to the Quaker church.

Cornelius Heathcote 1754 – 1825

Cornelius, John's eldest son, was just 7 years old when William Watson became his step-father, and he, his mother and siblings ceased to attend Quaker Meetings. However, it is worth recording the influence his stepfather had on him. As soon as he was old enough, he was taken into partnership with his step-father along with William and Edward Salisbury. Their ship *Molly* in 1760 – 1765 made 5 voyages between Sierra Leon and Charleston, Grenada and Barbados. On each voyage it carried between 200 and 230 enslaved Africans. [11] This was just as Cornelius was moving from childhood into adulthood. In all, his step-father had shares in 8 enslaving ships, most making multiple journeys from Lancaster or Liverpool. Watson and his associates transported 3,032 enslaved people between 1758 and 1803.

In 1782, aged 28, Cornelius inherited Barlborough Hall and the estate in Derbyshire from his father's older unmarried brother, Sir Gilbert Heathcote Reaston-Rodes. He moved from Lancaster and the influence of his stepfather. He added the family name of Reaston-Rodes to his name and died unmarried on 06 March 1825. [12]

It is of interest that he was succeeded at Barlborough Hall by Rev. Cornelius Heathcote Reaston-Rodes, who in 1826 owned a part share in a plantation called Quakers Hall in the Demerara district of British Guyana which in 1826 had 136 (58 female and 78 male) enslaved people working on it growing cotton. Brothers John and Robert Dodson of Lancaster had also been part owners of this estate at one stage. John and Robert Dodson, originally from Ulverston, were not Quakers. As Master Mariners, they captained enslaving ships out of Lancaster. The original owner of Quakers Hall appears to have been Samuel Kendal of Edinburgh. [13] It has not been possible to determine why the plantation was given this name.

Dodshon Foster 1730 – 1793

Dodshon Foster painted by William Tate displayed in the Maritime Museum Lancaster

Dodshon was the son of Robert (a Quaker Merchant) and Elizabeth Foster (neé Dodshon) of Hawthorne Durham. It is not clear when he came to Lancaster but, as a teenager, he would have met Lancaster Quakers at General and Yearly Meetings.

In 1737, he had inherited £900 from his Great Uncle Robert Foster a merchant in Rotterdam (£169,900 in 2024.) He inherited a further £120 from his Grandfather Nicholas Foster in 1751 (£22,799 in 2024.) [14]

He entered the enslaving industry in Lancaster in 1752 when just 21 years of age with John Heathcote. [15] His family did not traffic enslaved people in the way that John's had, so one could speculate that John was the one to suggest this partnership. That year, he became a Free Burgess, a young age to be admitted. [16] His inheritances clearly supported him in investments of land on the Quay in Lancaster and in ships with John Heathcote.

In 1753, Dodshon and Elizabeth Birket the daughter of Myles Birket, a Quaker Merchant and Banker, took each other in marriage at Lancaster Meeting House. Thus, he gained access to Myles' contacts in the West Indies and, through the Quaker Meeting, access to the dealings of other Quaker Merchants. They had four children: Robert in 1754, James in 1756, Myles in 1759, and Elizabeth in 1764. James died in childhood and Myles aged 21 in 1780.

We have already seen that with his Quaker partner John Heathcote and Captain Richard Millerson, he owned the Lancaster merchant and enslaving ship *Barlborough* and had shares in the *Bold* owned by Heathcote & Co.

I can find no record of either John Heathcote or Dodshon Foster being challenged by the Meeting about having guns on their ship or about their enslaved people trading activity.

Between 1755 and 1758, Dodshon was a member of the Lancaster Port Commission. He built a house and warehouse on St George's Quay, next to the Custom House (now the Maritime Museum.)

Just one month after John Heathcote's death in April 1758, Dodshon sold the *Barlborough* at the Sun Hotel in Lancaster. Subsequently, he reverted to becoming a general colonial trader, making good profits on cargos of goods produced by the enslaved, thus continuing to take part in the enslaving industry. With his father-in-law, he also owned the ship *Hawke* which sailed between the West Indian islands and South Carolina in 1757. [17]

The timing of the sale of the *Barlborough* coincides with the London Yearly Meeting declaration in 1758 that trading in enslaved people was a direct violation of the 'Gospel order'. It is not clear if this was the reason why he gave up trading the enslaved or if it was the death of John Heathcote that year which precipitated his decision.

Little is known about his later career except that in 1759 he both supplied mahogany he had imported to the Lancaster furniture-making company Gillows and bought furniture from them. It is suggested that he made sufficient money so that he no longer needed to be as heavily involved in colonial trading. In fact, in 1766 his diary tells us that he accompanied Elizabeth, who was by now very ill, on an extended visit to Bristol where she took the waters. They met up with the Gurneys, the Quaker Banking family from Norfolk, an uncle and cousins. Dodshon documented this visit in his diary, now in the Lancaster Museum Service archive, in great detail including the details of Elizabeth's symptoms along with all his expenses. [18]

Elizabeth died later that year and in 1772, Dodshon moved out of the house on the Quay to Parvus Hall on what is now Westbourne Road in Lancaster.

By this time Dodshon had become a pillar of the Quaker Meeting attending Monthly Meeting and was regularly being appointed to carry out tasks for the meeting. For example, in the March 1785 Minutes, we see that he was appointed, with Joshua Robinson, to draw up the answers to London Yearly Meeting Queries and the report on the completion of the inquiries within the meeting concerning 'Friends involved in the Slave Trade.' The minutes state that:

'The London Yearly Meeting Queries were read & answered by the representatives, and the following Friends were appointed to draw up answers consistent therewith to go to the Quarterly meeting. To be produced at the next Meeting for its approval Dodshon Foster & Joshua Robinson to whom it is on instruction that they make in the said anyway. The Completion of the visit to families was also the result of the inquiry of the London Yearly Meeting concerning the Slave Trade.' [19]

The appointment makes startling reading given his involvement in the enslaving industry until 1758. One would have thought that his previously known involvement in this would have meant that he would be considered an inappropriate Friend to be asked to undertake this inquiry. Clearly, a possible conflict of interest was not a consideration for the Lancaster Quaker Monthly Meeting in 1785.

Dodshon was appointed as an Overseer but in 1792 he became too infirm to carry out the role. [20]

He died on 2nd January 1793 and is buried in the Meeting House grounds next to his grandson who had been given Dodshon's name.

In his Will made on 14th December 1789 and proved in the Prerogative Court of Canterbury at London on 4th March 1793, Dodshon bequeathed to his son Robert £100. As Robert had been so well provided for in his grandfather Myles Birkett's Will, and on Robert's recommendation, the whole of the rest of his estate was left to his daughter Elizabeth.

Robert Foster 1754 – 1827

Dodshon and Elizabeth's surviving son Robert's life is of interest. He spent seven or eight years at the school of John Jenkinson, of Yealand Conyers, where he acquired 'a good English education and the rudiments of classical knowledge.' He then attended the Free School at Sedbergh.

His parents had decided that he might be a physician but he was not interested and, aged 18 years, went to sea. He made three voyages to the West Indies with Captain Roper on the *Marquis of Rockingham*. These voyages are not listed on the Voyages Database so one must assume they were colonial trading voyages. In 1772, he was apprenticed as a storekeeper in St John's, Antigua by his maternal grandfather Myles and great-uncle James Birket. He lived amongst the enslaved in the towns and frequently went to the plantations to collect debts and visit the managers thus seeing for himself the conditions endured by the enslaved on the plantations. In 1774, after paying a short visit to Lancaster, he went again with Capt. Roper for the last time to Antigua. By March 1775, he was on the *Dolphin*, bound for Dominica. [21]

Robert later joined the Royal Navy much to the dismay of his parents and Lancaster Quaker Preparative Meeting. It is interesting that he was not disowned despite joining a war ship, *Endeavour*, a ship that saw action against the Privateers in the West Indies. He went on to serve on a number of Royal Navy ships. It is said that between 1772 and 1778, he visited Dominique, Grenada, and all the British islands of the West Indies except Jamaica.

In 1779, Robert left his naval career. His uncle James Birket recording in his diary on
3rd November that year 'Robert Foster came home this morning after a long fighting campaign in sundry Men of War. He quit the fighting trade at his grandfather's request and seems to be a very sensible youth.'

Whilst visiting his grandfather in Sedbergh in 1780 Robert had renewed his acquaintance with Mary Burton, the daughter of the family with whom he had lodged when being educated at the Free School there. He became the manager of his grandfather's estate Hebblethwaite in 1781, living on the farm there with Mary as his housekeeper. Eventually in May 1781, he was visited by Friends from the Lancaster Monthly Meeting and questioned about his service in the Navy. No action was taken.

Robert and Mary married in 1784 at Brigflatts Quaker Meeting House Sedbergh. They had 8 children: Dodshon 1786; James 1787; Twins Elizabeth & John 1788; Mary 1790; Jane 1794; Isabel 1796; and Sarah 1797. [22]

In 1783, he inherited The Wood, the estate at Cartmel of his great uncle James Birket. In 1785, he inherited the two estates of his Grandfather Myles Birket, Hebblethwaite. Hall Sedbergh and Scarthwaite Lancaster. These properties had been developed by the Birket brothers who were very successful colonial traders, trading in goods produced by the enslaved and thus supporting the enslaving industry.

Robert settled his family in Hebblethwaite Hall and bought a further estate, Dove Gill, in 1787. Here we again see how the wealth derived from the sale of goods produced by the enslaved enhanced the lives of future generations. Despite his wealth, he dressed in the simple clothing of a workman in Quaker grey and was often mistaken for a person of that class by those who did not know him.

'For the better employment of the poor' in 1790, he built Hebblethwaite Mill in the Valley of Rawthey near Cautley. The mill prepared wool fleeces. It housed some of the first carding machines powered by a water wheel in the area. Initially, the carded wool was sent out to local families to be spun before being woven or knitted by hand. Spinning frames and then machines to wash and finish cloth were installed. [23] This is a clear example of money accrued from the enslavement industry being used to provide an operation set up to be a form of welfare project, the provision of paid employment preserving the dignity of those described as 'the poor.'

Once spinning was introduced, he took Joseph Dover into partnership and made him the manager. The spun yarn was sent out to local people's homes to be knitted into garments.

Joseph Dover and his sons amassed sufficient funds to establish their own woollen mill in 1837 on a bend in the river Clough just outside Sedbergh. They produced a garment just for the plantations in the West Indies, demonstrating how the enslavement industry became embedded in the British Woollen industry. [24]

In 1791, at the request of William Wilberforce MP, the abolitionist, Robert gave evidence before the Select Committee of the House of Commons on the Slave Trade, outlining his experiences of the treatment of the enslaved people he had encountered in the West Indies.

In 1799, Mary died. Robert married Margaret Burton, the widow of his first wife's brother, at Brigflatts in 1802. He was described on the marriage record as a Yeoman of Hebblethwaite Hall, West Riding, Yorkshire. During the following years, he became friends with William Wordsworth who stayed at Hebblethwaite and Samuel Taylor Coleridge.

Due to failing health, he sold the mill and his estates in February 1813. Hebblethwaite Hall, Scarthwaite, Gill House, Burnt Mill, and Dovecoat Gill estates were all sold by auction at the Kings Arms in Sedbergh to Warwick Pearson, Esq. of Kirby Lonsdale, for £10,800 (£628,029 in 2024). The Wood was sold to John Wakefield II of Kendal for £5,000 (£290,754 in 2024). He was the eldest son of Quaker John Wakefield who was disowned for supplying gunpowder to the 'Africa Trade.'

Robert moved to 53 Northumberland Street Newcastle in 1813 to be near his eldest son Myles a timber merchant and his family. [25]

He represented Newcastle Quaker Preparative Meeting at Monthly Meetings and was a frequent attendee at the London Yearly Meeting, combining this with visiting his son James, who lived there. He promoted the education of the poor in Newcastle.

In March 1824, he was a signatory to an open letter to the Mayor of Newcastle, requesting that he call a meeting for the purpose of petitioning Parliament for the 'Improvement and Gradual Emancipation of the Slave Population of the British Colonies.'

He died at his house in Northumberland Street on the 15th of June 1827 and was buried in the old graveyard in Pilgrim Street, Newcastle. He left £4,000 (£354,339 in 2024) to his extended family. He had already divested himself of a significant part of his wealth from the sale of his properties in 1813 by giving his two sons and son-in-law 'shares and effects.'

The Newcastle Courant, on the 23rd of June, 1827, reported his death as follows:

'He was a man of extensive literary and classical attainments, remarkable for his unaffected humility, his inflexible integrity, and for the sincerity and simplicity of his character. He was particularly careful not to speak evil of anyone and equally so in discouraging this practice in others. In fulfilling all the social duties of private life, he was a bright example, and his memory will long be cherished and revered by a numerous circle of friends.'

One has the impression from Robert's life that he was not entirely comfortable in inheriting the wealth from his grandfather and uncle, the wealth he knew had been gained from the labour of enslaved people. It could be that the knowledge he had of his father's involvement in the enslavement industry played a part in his suggestion to his father that he did not need to inherit from him.

REFERENCES

1. www.findmypast.co.uk/education&work British County Apprentices 1710-1808
2. Derbyshire Record Office D505 Rhodes family of Barlborough/Administrative History. https://calmview.derbyshire.gov.uk/CalmView?Record.aspx?src=Catalogue&id=D505
3. The Slave Trade and the Economic Development of Eighteenth-Century Lancaster 1992– Melinda Elder Page 127
4. Rolls of Freemen of the Borough of Lancaster 1688 – 1840 Vol 87 page 147
5. Lancaster Central & North Area Quaker Meeting Archive FRL2/1/5/30 - Disownments - John Heathcote & Millicent Satterthwaite, 1753 - 1754
6. www.slavevoyages.org/voyages/database
7. Melinda Elder: Dodson Foster of Lancaster and the West Indies (1730 -93) - Maritime Journal Vol 1. Pages 14-5.

8. The Slave Trade and the Economic Development of Eighteenth-Century Lancaster 1992– Melinda Elder Page 147
9. www.findmypast.co.uk/parishdeaths England & Wales, Society of Friends (Quaker) Burials 1578-1841
10. Lancaster Monthly Meeting Minute Book 1761 1st day of 6th Month LC&NAQM Archive FRL2/1/1/2
11. www.slavevoyages.org/voyages/database
12. Barlborough Heritage Centre www.barlboroughrc.chessck.co.uk/villagelife/interestingfacts
13. University College London Legacies of the British Slave Trade Data Base www.ucl.ac.uk/lbs/
14. The Foster Family of Cold Hesledon, Hawthorne, Lancaster and Sedbergh. Benjamin S Beck 2000- 2022 www.benbeck.co.uk
15. The Slave Trade and the Economic Development of Eighteenth-Century Lancaster 1992– Melinda Elder Page 127
16. Rolls of Freemen of the Borough of Lancaster 1688 – 1840 Vol 87 Page 111
17. The Foster Family of Cold Hesledon, Hawthorne, Lancaster and Sedbergh. Benjamin S Beck 2000- 2022 www.benbeck.co.uk
18. The diary is held in the Lancaster Maritime Museum, and this information was transcribed by Benjamine S Beck for The Foster Family of Cold Hesledon, Hawthorne, Lancaster and Sedbergh.
19. Lancaster Central & North Area Quaker Meeting Archive FRL 2/1/1/9 Monthly Meeting Minute Book 7 Apr. 1777 - 7 May 1787
20. Lancaster Central & North Area Quaker Meeting Archive FRL 2/1/1/11 Monthly Meeting Minute Book 6 Dec. 1790 - 9 Jan. 1797, including minutes for Lancaster Particular Meeting.
21. The Foster Family of Cold Hesledon, Hawthorne, Lancaster and Sedbergh. Benjamin S Beck 2000- 2022 www.benbeck.co.uk
22. www.findmypast.co.uk/parishmarriages/parishbirths England & Wales, Society of Friends (Quaker) 1578 – 1841
23. Out of Oblivion http://www.outofoblivion.org.uk/record.asp?id=276
24. Fairfield Mill Sedbergh Display Board 2022
25. Some Account of the Pedigree of the Fosters of Cold Hesledon – Joseph Foster 1862 – Forgotten Books.

THE SATTERTHWAITE; TOWNSON; DILLWORTH & RAWLINSON FAMILIES

The four Quaker families of Townson, Satterthwaite, Dillworth and Rawlinson, who were heavily involved in the colonial trade and enslavement industry, were, in fact, so connected by business partnerships and marriage that they could be seen as one trading unit. Millicent Satterthwaite's marriages with John Heathcote in 1753 and William Wilson in 1761 put them into family relationships with other Lancaster traders in enslaved people. Abigail Rawlinson's marriage in 1771 to William Lindow, an enslaving ship captain and plantation owner, gave access to plantations. Miles Barber, who became a Lancaster enslaver, was apprenticed to William Satterthwaite and John Heathcote was apprenticed to Thomas Satterthwaite.

Whilst some were involved in trafficking the enslaved, some also owned the enslaved by virtue of being part owners of plantations. All were involved in the colonial trade, which depended on the labour of the enslaved in the West Indies and America to provide the goods transported back to Lancaster for sale in the shops of these Lancaster merchants and beyond, principally tobacco, sugar, mahogany & raw cotton.

The records of the passage of ships are not clear and it may be that more ships than identified were owned by Lancaster Merchants primarily engaged in the colonial trade and/or engaged in secondary trading of the enslaved. This was moving the enslaved between the islands of the West Indies and America. The captains were charged with maximising income from their journeys and secondary slaving was a good way of keeping a ship loaded with 'cargo' as it moved between the islands and main land to gather goods to return to Lancaster.

The business relationships of these families and with those of other Quaker families are clear. The purchase document for Lots no. 18 & 21 on St George's Quay Lancaster on 25th January 1752 shows the signatures and seals of Abraham Rawlinson, Myles Birket, Robert Lawson, and Thomas Satterthwaite. They were all Port Commissioners.

A notebook from 1792, held in the archive of Lancaster City Museum Service, contains the names of the subscribers to the building of the Lancaster Kendal Canal.

Five members of the Rawlinson family are recorded on this page with four members of the Satterthwaite family. Others are recorded elsewhere in the book.

The Kendal Quaker John Wakefield, gunpowder mill owner, is also listed on this page.

The sums shown give an indication of the spare money available to the Rawlinsons for investment. The £5,000 invested by each of Thomas Rawlinson, Abraham Tyzack Rawlinson and his twin Henry Lindow Rawlinson in 1792 equates to £1,874,881 in 2024. These huge sums earned from the trading of enslaved people, the ownership of plantations on which the enslaved were forced to work and the sale of goods produced by them demonstrate how that money flowed back into the British economy and was used to build infrastructure to support businesses in Lancashire.

For each member of these four families, there follows a brief biography explaining what it has been possible to glean about their trading activity and relationships with the Quaker Monthly and Preparative Meetings.

Table 6.1 LINKS BETWEEN THE SATTERTHWAITE; TOWNSON; DILLWORTH; RAWLINSON & OTHER COLONIAL & SLAVE TRADING FAMILIES.

William Satterthwaite 1658 - 1717

- **Thomas Satterthwaite** 1685 – 1728; 1712 Married Ann Cannanby died 1714. 1716 Married Mary Ledger.
  - **William Satterthwaite** 1713 – 1808?; 1740 Married Martha Moss.
    - **John Satterthwaite** 1743 – 1807
  - **Benjamin Satterthwaite** 1718-92; 1741 married Jane Casson
    - **Cornelius Heathcote** 1754 – 1825
  - **Thomas Satterthwaite** 1720-90/1750 married Hannah Wilson
  - **Millicent Satterthwaite** 1728 – 66; married John Heathcote 1730 – 1758; 1761 married William Watson
- **Cecile Satterthwaite** 1682 - 1758; 1712 Married John Dillworth 1691 – 1747
  - **Thomas Dillworth** 1713 -86 married Sarah Shiers
  - **William Dillworth** 1716 -89 married Ester Shiers

Abraham Rawlinson 1666-1737 Married Elizabeth Beck 1670 - 1750

- **Thomas Hutton Rawlinson** 1712 – 69 married Mary Dilworth 1714 - 1786
  - **Abraham Rawlinson MP** 1738-1803
    - **Abigail Rawlinson** 1740 – 91 married William Lindow
    - **Henry Rawlinson MP** 1743-86 married Martha Tyzak
  - **John Rawlinson** 1741 - 99
    - **John Rawlinson** 1744-81 married Jane Hodgson
    - **Thomas Rawlinson** 1751 – 1802 married Sarah Cowell
  - **Thomas Hutton** 1752 - 77; 1776 married Hannah Satterthwaite
- **Abraham Rawlinson** 1709 -80 married Elling Godslave

THE DILLWORTH FAMILIES

John Dillworth 1690 -1747

The birth of John Dillworth, son of Thomas and Mary Dillworth of Bradley Hall, is recorded as 16 January 1690 in the Lancaster Quaker Records. He came from Wyresdale. His family were Flaxmen (men who grew and treated flax to be woven into linen garments.) The Lancaster Quarterly Meeting Book of Sufferings, which records the seizures of goods from Quakers for non-payment of tithe and other Anglican dues, shows that members of the family were engaged in the flax trade for over a hundred and fifty years. [1]

On the 18th November 1712, John and Cecile Satterthwaite took each other in marriage at Colthouse Meeting House, Hawkshead. [2]

This marriage brought John into contact with Miles Townson, who became his brother-in-law and, through him, the Rawlinsons and their enslaving business. The Dillworth family history labels John as a 'slave trader'. Later his sons Thomas and William were drawn into the business by their involvement with the Rawlinson family.

In 1721-2, John was admitted as a Free Burgess of Lancaster. In this record, he is still classed as a Flaxman. [3]

In 1732, he took an apprentice, Thomas Albright, into the business. Once more, the documentation refers to John as a 'flax dresser.' The apprentice premium was £50 (£10,360 in 2024). A second apprentice, John Ecroyd, was taken in 1745. His premium was £30 (£5,965 in 2024.) In this record, John is now described as a Merchant. By 1745, the business was described as 'John Dilworth and Sons'. [4] They became involved in shipping goods. (The family name is spelt as Dilworth in some documents and Dillworth in others. The spelling used in this book follows the spelling used by William when he signs his name on Quaker documents unless quoting.)

In 1737, John was a large subscriber to 'The Buoy Account', and his sons Thomas and William were auditors. Here, we have a ship owner ensuring safe passage for his ships into Lancaster. John Dillworth and Sons were in partnership with the Rawlinson brothers, Abraham and Thomas Hutton, and Miles Townson in taking a further apprentice. The Lancaster Freeman and Apprentice Books also show us that they were co-owners of the ship *Recovery*:

> '18 November & 19 November 1746 John Dilworth and Sons and Co., owners of the ship *Recovery*; two entries both signed T. H. Rawlinson.' [5]

It is not clear if this ship was involved in the colonial trade or trafficking the enslaved from Africa from the material available. Still, his partnership with Rawlinson would have brought him into contact with the latter.

In 1739, John was the Cashier of the Lancaster Quaker Meeting, collecting the annual subscriptions and himself giving 7 shillings and 6 pence (£187.33 in 2024)[6]. That year, he provided a new Weight House and Crane for the Customs House on the Quay to assist local merchants. He was clearly doing well in business.

John died on 11 November 1747, aged 56 and is buried in the grounds of the Meeting House. His death is recorded under that of Miles Townson in the Monthly Meeting Records. There is no record of probate being granted for a Will.

After John's death, Thomas and William took over the business. They are described variously as merchants, flax dressers or shipowners.

Thomas Dillworth 1713 – 86 & William Dillworth 1716 – 89

Thomas, with his brother William, had become established colonial traders in Lancaster, trading in goods produced by enslaved people so taking advantage of the emerging enslaving industry.

Both brothers were admitted as Free Burgesses of Lancaster. Thomas in 1731/2 and William in 1732/3.[7]

On 19 February 1740, Thomas and Sarah Shiers, the daughter of Quakers William Shiers and Sarah Storrs of Manningham near Bradford, took each other in marriage at Brighouse Quaker Meeting House in Yorkshire. They had eight children, 5 boys and 3 girls, of whom only three survived to adulthood: John 1745 - 1830; Lydia b1746 who married William Jepson; and Joseph b1749 who was killed in 1773, aged 24, 'shot by a fowling piece'.[8]

On 19 November 1742, William and Esther Shiers, Sarah's older sister, took each other in marriage also at Brighouse. They had seven children, five girls and two sons. Only four of the girls lived beyond infancy: Ester b1746, who married Quaker Merchant David Dockray; Cecily b1748, who married Thomas Crewdson; Mary b1753 and Sarah b1754.

William was clearly well-respected. In 1747 he was executor of the Will of Miles Townson, his uncle by marriage.

In 1752, the ship *Providence* left Barbados for South Carolina with 'twenty new negros'(sic) on board.[9] The Dillworth brothers were part owners of this ship with Abraham and Thomas Hutton Rawlinson. This was termed secondary slave trading. It could be that until the vessel returned to Lancaster, this activity was not known to the Dillworths. Their captain would have been responsible for maximising the income on this voyage. So, the transporting of the enslaved in this way could have been his way of maintaining an income stream throughout the ship's time between Barbados and South Carolina.

Together, the brothers took apprentices. In 1754, Samuel Bradford was taken for a premium of £45 (£8,048 in 2024) and in this record, they are termed Flaxmen. Then, in 1768, Edward Rigg was taken for a premium of £10 (£1,415 in 2024.) Here, they are said to be Merchants. At some point in this period, William became a banker. It is not clear when but he is described as such in several records. It is very likely that his banking business had amongst its clients the Rawlinsons and Satterthwaites and other Quaker Merchants and enslavers of Africans.

The brothers, in particular William, played a significant part in the life of the local Quaker Meetings. William was an Elder and, at Meeting for Sufferings in 1757, presented the report of the Elders and Ministers. At that meeting, the following minute expressing concern that some Quakers were dealing in negros and asking for previous minutes about the slave trade to be sent out was made and sent to Quaker Meetings across Britain and the Colonies:

'This meeting being apprehensive that some under our name both in this Nation and in the Colonies abroad are concerned for .... in dealing in Negros. The Meeting for Sufferings is desired to send copies of several minutes of the meeting relating thereto, and also extracts of such advices from our printed Epistles on that subject, to the several Counties of this Nation & the Colonies abroad for their Admonition, & also to give them each advice as may appear to them necessary.

A True Copy

Jacob Post Clerk' [10]

Thus, William was part of the group at the London Yearly Meeting discerning the response to trading in enslaved people in Britain and would surely have commented on this when back in Lancaster. Or was this too weighty a subject for discernment given the involvement of a significant group of his Lancaster Friends?

From 1761 - 1775, William was the Clerk of the of the Monthly Meeting's Ministers and Elders. In 1774, he followed his father in being appointed as the Cashier of the Preparative Meeting. In 1776, he became Clerk of the Quarterly Meeting, as evidenced in the record of the marriage of Thomas Hutton Rawlinson (Junior) and Hannah Satterthwaite, the daughter of Thomas Satterthwaite.

In 1767, Ester died. At Preston Patrick Meeting House in October 1770, William took a second wife, Quaker Mary Wakefield, a widow in membership of Kendal Meeting. She was the mother of John Wakefield, the gunpowder mill owner who was involved in supplying those involved in the 'Africa Trade' with gunpowder in Lancaster and Liverpool.

William served as an Elder in 1779, 1785 & 1786, despite his asking in April 1782 to lay down service 'due to old age coming on me a pace'. The meeting found it difficult to replace him in his many roles recording in June 1782 that they were still looking to appoint. Despite his request, he was appointed as a Minister in 1787, but in December of that year, he was 'considered to be incapable by indisposition of the body'. He was that year replaced as Cashier by John Field, a grocer in Lancaster who, in later years moved to Liverpool and became a tea merchant.

William died in April 1789 and was buried in the Friends Burying Ground Lancaster. Probate was granted in July 1789.

William's older brother Thomas played a lesser role in the meeting but was part of the group of Friends appointed in 1775 to investigate the expansion of Lancaster Meeting House and was a regular representative of the Lancaster Preparative Meeting to Monthly Meetings.

The Liverpool Plantation Registers 6th – 11th October 1773 record the *Lively* of Jamacia, an enslaving ship owned by the Rawlinson brothers and their sons along with Thomas Dillworth and his son John with a capacity for 270 enslaved.[11] Thus, we have clear evidence that Thomas was involved in trafficking the enslaved.

Thomas died in April 1786. The instruction to the grave digger William Knowles records that Thomas was no longer a member of the Monthly Meeting but there seems to be no evidence in the archive that he was disowned.

Probate was granted in July 1786.

John Dillworth (Junior) 1745 – 1830

In 1776, Thomas's son John, born in 1745, married Sarah Arthington, the daughter of a Leeds Banker. John founded a Bank in Lancaster in 1794. His partners were Robert Morley Arthington and Robert Birkett, both Quakers and, in Robert Arthington's case, a relative by marriage. John ran the bank until it failed in February 1826 due to a run on the bank. John, now 81, and his partners were declared bankrupt; the proven debts were £145,835, (in 2024 £12,125,526). The three Quakers are described in the bankruptcy notices in the London Gazette as Bankers, Dealers and Chapmen (Merchants or Traders). [12]

Lancaster Quaker Monthly Meeting was clearly acutely embarrassed by this very public failure. They held an inquiry. Given the likely hood that a significant number of Quakers had lost money, this is not surprising. The investigation found that no balance sheets had been kept for 4 years and that John's 'faculties and memory having much failed' had contributed to the mismanagement. [13]

John died in 1830, aged 85. He was living in Yealand but is buried in Lancaster.

John and Sarah's daughter Mary, born in 1777 married Joshua Gilpin, a paper manufacturer of Pennsylvania, in 1800 at Yealand Meeting House. Their eldest son, Henry Dilworth Gilpin and Thomas's Gt Grandson, born in Yealand in 1801, became the Attorney General for the United States in 1840.

Postscript

In October 1783, there is recorded at Lancaster St Mary's Anglican Church the baptism of William Dillworth, an adult negro.[14]

Was he the servant of William Dillworth? If so, why was he baptised at St. Mary's? Or was he a second black servant of Abraham Rawlinson, given the name of William, who was the chief instigator of the inquiry which resulted in the Testimony of Denial disowning Abraham and his brother John in November 1779. We may never know.

REFERENCES

1. MM Scholfield Letter Book of Benjamin Satterthwaite. Page 127
2. www.findmypast.co.uk/parishmarriages   England & Wales, Society of Friends (Quaker) 1578 – 1841
3. Rolls of Freemen of the Borough of Lancaster 1688 – 1840 Vol 87 Page 92
4. www.findmypast.co.uk/education&work British County Apprentices 1710-1808
5. MM Schofield - The Letter Book of Benjamin Satterthwaite of Lancaster 1737-1744 Page131 (1960)
6. Lancaster Central & North Area Quaker Meeting Archive FRL 3/1/1/1 Minute Book 1678 - 1740
7. The Record Society of Lancashire and Cheshire Vol 87 Page 92

8. www.findmypast.co.uk/parishburials England & Wales, Society of Friends (Quaker) 1578 – 1841
9. The Slave Trade and Economic Development of Eighteenth-Century Lancaster. M. Elder 1992 - Ryburn Academic M. Elder- The Slave Trade - Page 116
10. Lancaster Central & North Area Quaker Meeting Archive FRL 21/1/1/31 London Yearly Meeting Minutes 1757
11. MM Schofield Letter Book of Benjamin Satterthwaite 1960 Pages 131/2
12. London Gazette (1665 – 2018) 1827 edition 2483 in www.findmypast.co.uk/newspapers
13. Lancaster Central & North Area Quaker Meeting Archive - Monthly Meeting Minutes 10 May 1826 FRL 2/1/1/17 & Report FRL2/1/19/9
14. www.findmypast.co.uk/parishbaptisms

THE SATTERTHWAITE FAMILIES

Table 8.1

SATTERTHWAITE FAMILY TREE

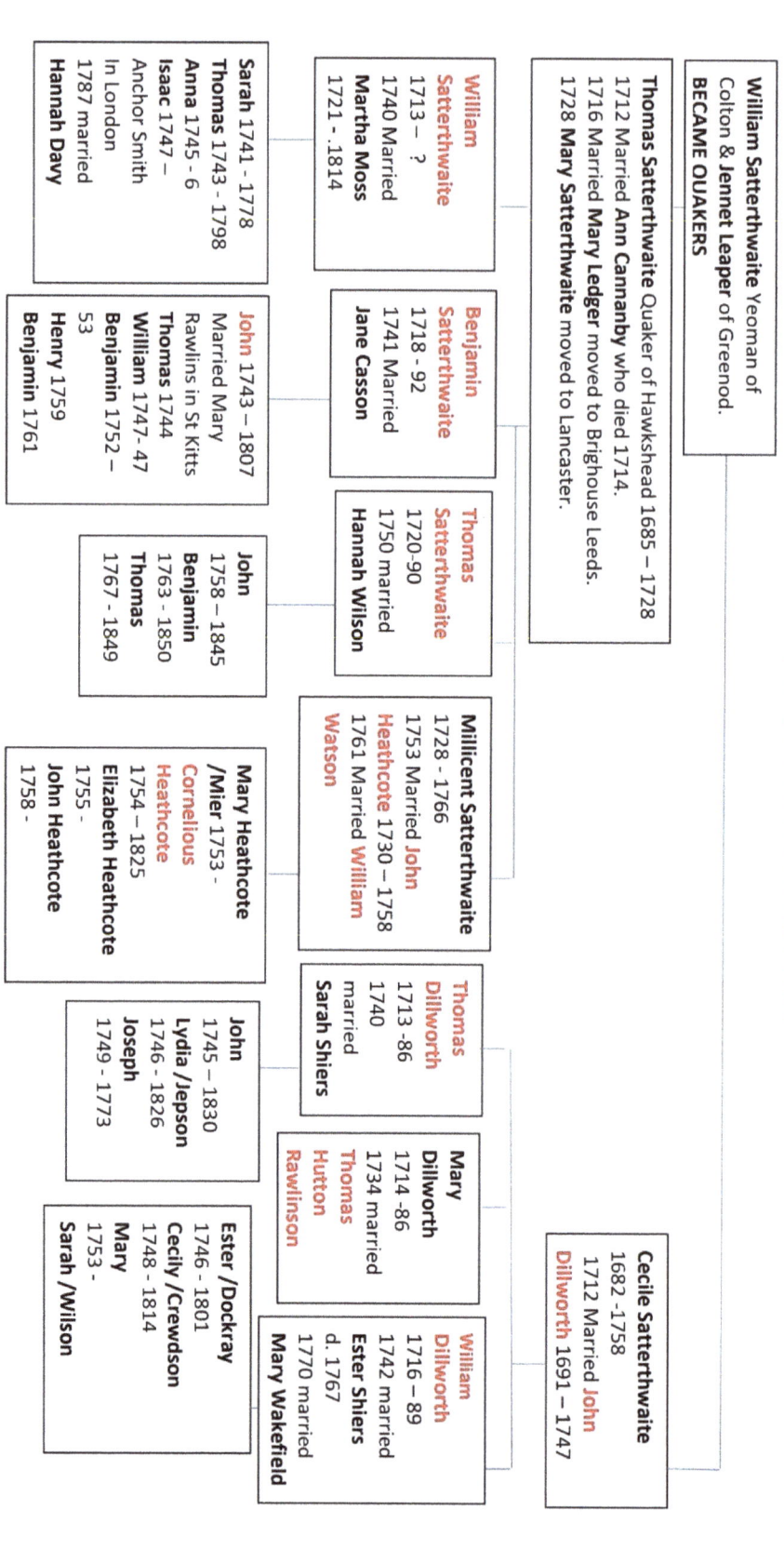

William Satterthwaite 1713 – ?

Born 3rd February 1713, William was the only child of Thomas Satterthwaite and Ann Cannanby who died in 1714. His parents were both Quakers. William's early life was in Hawkshead but when his father remarried Mary Ledger in 1716 they moved to Brighouse, Yorkshire. His father died there in 1728.

Mary Satterthwaite moved her family to Lancaster. Thomas's sister Cecily had married John Dillworth in 1712 and lived in Lancaster. So after Thomas's death in 1728 it is not surprising that Millicent, with two young children, moved to be near this family. William, her step son, was by now 15 and it is likely that he was placed in an apprenticeship by his Uncle John with one of the Quaker Merchants in the city.

When William was admitted as Free Burgess in 1736/7 he was classed as an Ironmonger, [1] an occupation he retained when he married. It is likely that he was apprenticed to one of the five Quaker Ironmongers in the city but, as the apprenticeship records do not start until 1736, we cannot tell which of them it was. William Stout, an obvious Quaker ironmonger to be an apprentice's master, makes no mention of William in his autobiography.

William and Martha Moss took each other in marriage on 22 October 1740 in Warrington Quaker Meeting House. Martha, born 19 February 1721, was the daughter of Isaac (a hosier) and Sarah Moss of Manchester. Their marriage was witnessed by a good number of Lancaster Quakers. They included William's mother Mary (now Townson), William and John Dillworth and Thomas Hutton Rawlinson. [2] This marriage related William to the Lawson family.

In 1742 William took an apprentice, James Gosling, at a premium of £60.0s. (£11,052 in 2024.) By 1749, when Miles Barber became his apprentice, the premium was £100.00s. (£18,493 in 2024.) These were very large sums of money which William was able to invest in his business. William was still classed as an Ironmonger in these records. [3] Miles Barber was to become a trader of enslaved people and eventually owner of the enslaving ship *Gambia*. He was not a Quaker.

We know that William was in partnership with his stepfather Miles Townson. Together they owned the ship *Martha,* presumably named after William's wife, as was the custom. [4] William was involved in other partnerships. MM Schofield, in his paper 'The Letter Book of Benjamin Satterthwaite of Lancaster 1737-1744 '*(1960),* references:

'Miss E. Donnan's printed letters *(pp. cit.,* Vol. 4, pp. 335-344 *passim)* from
Henry Laurens of Charleston, S. Carolina, 1755-6, which refers to slaves sold
there from the *Gambia,* owned by "Satterthwaite and Inman", wrongly identified by Miss Donnan as "of Liverpool". Some of the slaves had been sent from Barbados by the firm of "Law, Satterthwaite and Jones". The proceeds of the sale of the slaves were remitted at the firm's request by a bill of exchange to Samuel Touchet of London. The Satterthwaite has not been identified, but Miss E. Donnan quoted Laurens's accounts in 1751 for slaves sold on behalf of William Satterthwaite.' (Vol. 4, pp. 306-8).

Thus we have evidence of William's involvement in dealing with enslaved Africans. In fact it was William's youngest stepbrother, Thomas, who was in partnership with Inman and his other stepbrother, Benjamin, who was in partnership with Law and Jones. [5]

By 1752 William had managed to get himself into debt. It is interesting to see the lengths to which Lancaster Quaker Monthly Meeting was prepared to go to help William with this problem as this extract from the Minute Book makes clear.

'Upon inquiry, if there be anything to offer this meeting upon the Queries Lancaster Meeting give Acct. that William Satterthwaite, a Member of their Meeting is in some danger of falling short in the payment of his just debts, but hath assigned over the whole of his Effects to Trustees for the benefit of his Creditors, agreeable to the advice of Friends. It is recommended to the care of Friends of Lancaster Meeting to see that all the satisfaction be given to his creditors, that the nature of his affairs will admit, and to report the care therein;- nothing further appears to be offered to this Meeting upon the Queries, the care continued.' [6]

Despite this, by 1758 William was again in debt. The minutes of the Monthly Meeting on the 6th day of the 11th month record that 'Great reproach is brought upon our Religious Profession' by his behaviour and he was again to be visited.

It was reported at the following meeting on the 4th of the 12th month that William could give no satisfactory account. A 'Testimony of Denial' against Wiliam was to be read at Lancaster Meeting after Meeting for Worship. Thus he was disowned by Lancaster Quakers for regularly getting into debt.

'The Friends appointed report; they visited William Satterthwaite, who could or would give no satisfactory Account for the deficiency in his outward concerns; Wherefore having prepared a few lines by way of Testimony against him, the same was read approved and signed by the Clerk by order & on behalf of this Meeting, And Friends before appointed are desired to give him a copy thereof, and afterwards it is ordered to be publicly read in Lancaster Meeting & further published as occasion may be observed.' [7]

He was not readmitted. I cannot be sure of the date of William's death but Martha died in 1814 aged 92 in Tamworth.

Benjamin Satterthwaite 1718 – 92

Portrait Benjamin Satterthwaite displayed in the Judges Lodgings Museum on loan from the family.

Benjamin was the first-born child of Quakers Thomas Satterthwaite and Mary Ledger on 9th June 1718 in Brighouse in Yorkshire. He became the step son of Miles Townson when he was 14 years of age. Miles greatly influenced his career.

In 1737, at the age of 19 Benjamin was sent to Barbados where, until June 1738, he learnt the role of being the representative of a group of Merchants in Lancaster who were trading goods with Barbados. He was Assistant Factor to Abraham Rawlinson from December 1739 until January 1741. Then he became the sole representative replacing Thomas Hutton Rawlinson, Abraham's younger brother. During this time he wrote frequently to his family, mainly his step father, Uncle John Dillworth and cousins in Lancaster, but also to other acquaintances. Many of these letters have been preserved by his descendants in a letter book held by the Lancaster City Library Service.

A good number of the ships leaving Lancaster stopped in Ireland to complete their cargo for the West Indies. For example, the Townson partners bought fifty barrels of beef from Captain Stephen Haven of Belfast which Benjamin received on 22nd July 1740. Hoare and Pike of Cork supplied butter and beef to the partners in August 1737 and in September 1739 butter to Lancaster Alderman John Casson.

Benjamin's role was to sell these and buy goods to send back. In carrying out these tasks Benjamin became very aware of the conditions endured by the enslaved in Barbados. In the Letter Book there is one letter to Captain William Day and there are many references to him in other letters. He was the owner of negros on his plantation Jambou Vale on St Vincent. Benjamin wrote on 20th October 1740 that because of the news of the arrival of a French fleet at Martinique:

"William Day is gone down to bring all his negros up" to Barbados.

Day appears in the letters more often as owner of at least two sloops in which he brought cotton from the islands down wind or to leeward of Barbados to be sold to complete the loading of ships already part filled with the heavy hogsheads of sugar.

In one letter, Benjamin wrote to Miles Townson:

"One of Captain Day's sloops came up yesterday by whom I have got as much cotton with what I had before as will serve the Content, and as thou orders in thy last to purchase all W. Day's [cotton], he is now turning up in the sight of the Island with as much as will serve the industry which I intend to buy." [8]

It is very likely that this cotton was sold to Manchester merchants to satisfy the burgeoning cotton manufacturing industry once it arrived in Lancaster.

In September 1741, Benjamin married Jane Casson, an Anglican and the daughter of Alderman Casson of Lancaster, who, through Miles Townson, had sent out goods to Barbados for Benjamin to sell. In deciding to 'marry out' and ignoring the Quaker Meeting and his parents, Benjamin was disowned by Friends in August 1741. The Lancaster Monthly Meeting Minutes declared that:

"Contrary to frequent advice, he accompanied a young woman not of our religion in order to marry her and notwithstanding advice has married by a priest upon which this meeting testifies him to be out of unity with us until he shew (sic) sincere remorse for his going out as aforesaid".

The "Testimony of Denial" drawn up by that meeting is to be read out at a subsequent Meeting for Worship was signed by seven Friends, including William Stout and John Dillworth. It adds to the previous report that Benjamin had so "slighted the tender and repeated advice of his parents and the approved rules of the Society as to marry privately by a priest a person of another persuasion". [9]

Following this, his family gave him no work. Benjamin's letter to Captain Thomas Greenup of Liverpool makes clear the problems he had following his marriage:

'Since I left your town, I have been at my [step] father Townson's several times who never offered me a birth though they're going to fit out a vessall [sic] for Barbados and another for Antigua. This is to advise you that I am still in the same mind and that if a birth fell out in your town for any part of the West Indies, I would embrace it with a great deal of pleasure if offered to me. I once more desire you'd make a little enquiry and see whether you think there'll be any vacant this year, or if you could give any incouragement [sic], that is if you think I might depend on one the next season. My father [law] Casson, with some others, will imploy [sic] me this year so as that I may be at liberty the latter end next summer, but if you don't think I might depend on one, they'll keep me in the same imployed [sic], I believe it's to follow the Jamaica trade. Had much rather sail from your town for several reasons.

I hope this will meet you and family well…' [10]

At this time Quakers were so persecuted by the Anglicans that they demanded a strong sense of unity that included a 'strong sense of remorse' for marrying out. Benjamin appears to have been unable to show this sense of remorse. Jane was the granddaughter of a Church Warden and niece of another so she may not have wished to follow Quaker discipline and become a Quaker. Benjamin and Jane remained Anglicans as did his descendants.

After his marriage Benjamin moved first to Liverpool and then back to Lancaster. Robert Gillow and his associates, the renowned furniture makers, employed Benjamin as their factor in Barbados between 1749 and 1751 to ship mahogany to Lancaster.

His letters from Jamaica hint at dealing in African cargo in the 1750s. This was probably his involvement with the Law, Satterthwaite and Jones partnership which dealt in the enslaved and, as outlined in Henry Lauren's letters in 1755/6, sent enslaved from Barbados to Charleston, South Carolina for sale. Laurens also sold the cargo of enslaved aboard the *Charming Nancy* for William Davenport of Liverpool in 1757.

By 1763 Benjamin was back in the employment of his family as a Factor in Jamaica. His letters suggest he had close links with Liverpool slaver captains.[11] In 1764 he agreed to sell an enslaved person for William Dingman of Liverpool, a person he first had to get well which he did at a cost to himself. This sale and the other evidence do suggest that Benjamin Satterthwaite was dealing in the enslaved in the 1750s. It is also clear that he bought and sold goods produced by the labour of the enslaved, profiting from the enslaving industry.

Benjamin presents a sad picture, a man who really failed in business, possibly in no small part due to his marrying out of the Quaker community in Lancaster.

John Satterthwaite 1743 – 1807

John Satterthwaite, the eldest of Benjamin Satterthwaite's sons, was not a Quaker. Still he provides another example of how these families remained intertwined in business despite Quaker disownments, providing excellent bases for their sons to make significant fortunes from enslaving.

John was also sent to Barbados as a Factor for Lancaster merchants who were buying commodities such as sugar, indigo and mahogany from the West Indies which he shipped to

Lancaster. He became a resident merchant in his own right on St Kitts where he married Mary Rawlins the daughter of a local plantation owner.

He returned to Lancaster a rich and successful merchant, bringing with him a female black servant. It is thought she was to keep his wife company and remind her of home in St Kitts. There is a baptismal record at St Mary's Lancaster dated 1778 of Frances Elizabeth Johnson, "a black woman servt. to Mr John Satterthwaite". [12]

Frances's age was given as 27 years. She lived with the family in the largest house on Castle Hill, Lancaster.

John Satterthwaite, painted by George Romney, displayed in the Judges Lodgings Lancaster also on loan from the family.

Little is known about Frances or Fanny as she was known. We do not know whether she married or had children, whether she was a "free" slave as many black servants in England at this time were regarded or whether she was paid for her work. There is no record of her death. The only thing that we have is the commemorative stone where her hand was buried in the Memorial Garden at St Mary's Church, now the Priory Church in Lancaster, close to the house where she had worked as a servant. The preserved hand, which had been kept in the Satterthwaite family for generations, was finally buried there in April 1997 by a descendant of the family, Eliza Dear, a Settle Meeting Quaker. Eliza had failed to get the authorities in St Kitts to repatriate it.

John's clerk, John Stout, wrote that his master made a large part of his fortune 'as a merchant in Lancaster between 1779 and 1785 so that he was able to retire in 1788'. [13]

An imagined portrait of Frances Elizabeth Johnson by Lela Harris 2022 displayed in the Judges Lodgings Lancaster Facing the Past Project.

The Voyages Database records that John was part owner of a number of enslaving ships:

The *Sisters* sailed from Liverpool in 1769 for Gambia, where 144 enslaved were embarked and trafficked to Charleston. 24 enslaved died on this journey.

In 1781, John wrote to his brokers about his ship *Sally*, '…she'll have a good deal of dead cargo (*elephant teeth and camwood*), and not but few slaves'.

The *Stag* for which his father assisted in providing goods to ship out according to his letters sailed from Liverpool on three voyages:

    1782 to Bonny trafficking 680 enslaved to St Lucia, of whom only 623 survived
    1783 from Bonny to Dominica, trafficking 655, of whom 600 survived
    1784 344 were trafficked from Bonny to Kingston Jamaica, 315 surviving [14]

John Satterthwaite trafficked 1,679 enslaved Africans from Bonny, Nigeria, of whom 141 died during the passage to the West Indies.

John became a very wealthy business man enabling him to buy the prime position at the crossing (where the choir, nave and transept intersect) in which to be buried in St Mary's Church in 1807.

Thomas Satterthwaite 1720 – 90

In 1739, when aged 19 Thomas was sent out to Barbados by his stepfather, Miles Townson, to join his brother Benjamin. He was to take:

"21 Thick Cheeses 4 cwt. 0 qu. 18lb. valued at £4. 0d." on his own and his mother Mary Townson's account for Benjamin to "dispose of and send us in return a little sugar and rum which I can dispose of better than cotton". [15]

This was to be the start of his career not just in the colonial trade but in trafficking in the enslaved. He was to be a much more successful businessman than either of his older brothers.

In 1742/3, he was made a Free Burgess of Lancaster and, in 1748, he took John Heathcote to be his apprentice at a premium of £100 (£18,420 in 2024). In 1753 John married Thomas's younger sister Millicent. Thomas is described as a Merchant in this documentation. From 1752 to 1767 Thomas Satterthwaite Merchant took 4 further apprentices at premiums ranging from £9. 9s to £210. 0s.0d (£1,824 - £31,595 in 2024.) These gave significant injections of money into his business. [16]

In 1747, Miles Townson named Thomas Satterthwaite in his Will as his "son-in-law and partner in trade" and his chief trustee. Thomas was, in fact, his stepson in today's parlance. He is named in his step father's partnerships, in the Apprentice Roles and the Liverpool Plantation Registers as part owner of the *Lively* of Jamaica which the Rawlinson family registered there as an enslaving ship.

In 1750, Thomas married Hannah Wilson of Kendal at Aldingham Parish Church. Thomas was disowned by the Lancaster Monthly Meeting for 'marrying out'.

During the period of his disownment, Thomas was in partnership with Charles Ingham, another factor in the West Indies. Melinda Elder suggests that they entered the slave trade in 1753. [17] Thus, at this time, he was not a member of the Religious Society of Friends but the Meeting's records make clear that he was still attending Meetings for Worship in Lancaster.

Satterthwaite and Ingham owned the *Swallow,* which sailed from Lancaster in 1754 to Gambia, trafficking 98 enslaved, of whom 77 disembarked in Barbados. [18]

In 1755, Thomas, in partnership with Charles, used their enslaving ship *Gambia* to move 15 enslaved Africans from Barbados to South Carolina.

On 27 August 1756, there was advertised for sale at Lancaster:

'The brigantine Swallow, burthen about 70 tons, with all her materials, as lately arrived from Africa and Barbados. She was built at Lancaster in the year 1751, is well found and of proper dimensions for the slave trade. For particulars apply to Messrs Satterthwaite and Inman in Lancaster.' [19]

In 1759, the *Marlborough,* owned by Thomas and Charles Ingham, sailed from Lancaster to Gambia. 200 enslaved were embarked and trafficked to Charleston, where 190 disembarked, 10 having died at sea. The *Marlborough* left Lancaster for Gambia again in 1760. On this voyage, 229 enslaved were trafficked to Charleston only 196 surviving the middle passage. [20]

Thus, whilst William & Benjamin were selling the enslaved, Thomas was concerning himself with the ownership of enslaving ships and trafficking the enslaved. This activity seems to have been rewarded as Thomas was elected as a Port Commissioner of Lancaster from 1758 – 1761. [21]

It was not until 1764 that Thomas 'Acknowledged Fault' to Lancaster Monthly Meeting for his unquakerly marriage. He was reinstated to membership on his application and acknowledgement of misconduct. His wife was admitted as a member at the same time. The notice of resumption of membership referred to their regular attendance at the Quaker Meeting for Worship despite his disownment. [22]

Clearly, the minutes of the London Yearly Meeting in 1761 were ignored as he was not formally 'laboured with' for his involvement in the Transatlantic Chattel Slave Trade and was, in fact, readmitted to membership whilst heavily involved in trafficking the enslaved. There is nothing in the archive to indicate that a visitation to Thomas was made by Monthly Meeting Friends to discuss his involvement.

The Satterthwaite Ingham partnership trafficked a total of 671 enslaved from Gambia, of whom 80 died at sea.

MM Schofield records that Thomas' Will, proved in 1792, shows that he had a considerable fortune; he stated his intention to treat his two sons and five daughters on the same basis as his son John, who had been given £1,500 on entering partnership with Joseph Bland. He lent a further £1,000 on bond, which bond was now to be cancelled. These bequests would require a sum of £17,500 (£2,182,570 in 2024). This equality of treatment was to be secured by a distribution of the profits of his shares in the Cark Cotton Mill of Thackray, Stockdale and Co., which must have been significant to provide so much; any additional income raised was to be distributed equally among the eight children.

Thus, through trafficking the enslaved and profiting from the manufacture of cotton goods using a raw material picked by the enslaved, Thomas Satterthwaite lived a very comfortable life and left his children and future generations able to do the same.

The three brothers had a difficult start in life, in William's case, losing both his parents while still a child. For Benjamin and Thomas, the loss of their father and, for all, being moved to Lancaster and adjusting to a new stepfather must have been disruptive. They appear to have gone their separate ways unlike other Quaker families of that time but all by virtue of their Quaker connections became involved in the enslaving industry.

REFERENCES

1. The Record Society of Lancashire and Cheshire Vol 90 page 284
2. www.findmypast.co.uk/parishmarriages England & Wales, Society of Friends (Quaker) 1578 – 1841
3. www.findmypast.co.uk/education Britain County Apprentices 1710-1808
4. The Slave Trade and the Economic Development of Eighteenth-Century Lancaster 1992– Melinda Elder Page 118
5. The Slave Trade and the Economic Development of Eighteenth-Century Lancaster 1992– Melinda Elder Page 132
6. Lancaster Central & North Area Quaker Meeting Archive Ref: 2/1/1/2 Monthly Meeting Minute Book. Minutes of the Meeting held on 18th day of the 9th month of 1752
7. Lancaster Central & North Area Quaker Meeting Archive FRL 2/1/1/2 Monthly Meeting Minute Book 4th 12th 1758
8. The letter Book of Benjamin Satterthwaite – held in Lancaster City Library
9. The Letter Book of Benjamin Satterthwaite of Lancaster 1737-1744 - MM Schofield (1960) Pages 157-8
10. The Letter Book of Benjamin Satterthwaite of Lancaster 1737-1744 - MM Schofield (1960) Page 160
11. The Slave Trade and the Economic Development of Eighteenth-Century Lancaster 1992– Melinda Elder Page 213
12. www.findmypast.co.uk/parishbaptisms England & Wales, Society of Friends (Quaker) 1578 – 1841
13. Transactions of the Historic Society of Lancashire and Cheshire. Volume CX111
14. www.slavevoyages.org/voyages/database
15. The Letter Book of Benjamin Satterthwaite of Lancaster 1737-1744 - MM Schofield (1960) Page162
16. www.findmypast.co.uk/education&work/apprenticeships
17. The Slave Trade and the Economic Development of Eighteenth-Century Lancaster 1992– Melinda Elder Page 127
18. www.slavevoyages.org/voyages/database
19. The Slave Trade from Lancashire and Cheshire Ports Outside Liverpool c1750-c1790 MM Schofield, M.A. Page 31
20. www.slavevoyages.org/voyages/database
21. The Slave Trade and the Economic Development of Eighteenth-Century Lancaster 1992– Melinda Elder Page 182
22. Lancaster Central & North Area Quaker Meeting Archive reference: FRL/2/1/4/9

THE RAWLINSON FAMILIES

Table 9.1

RAWLINSON DECENDANTS

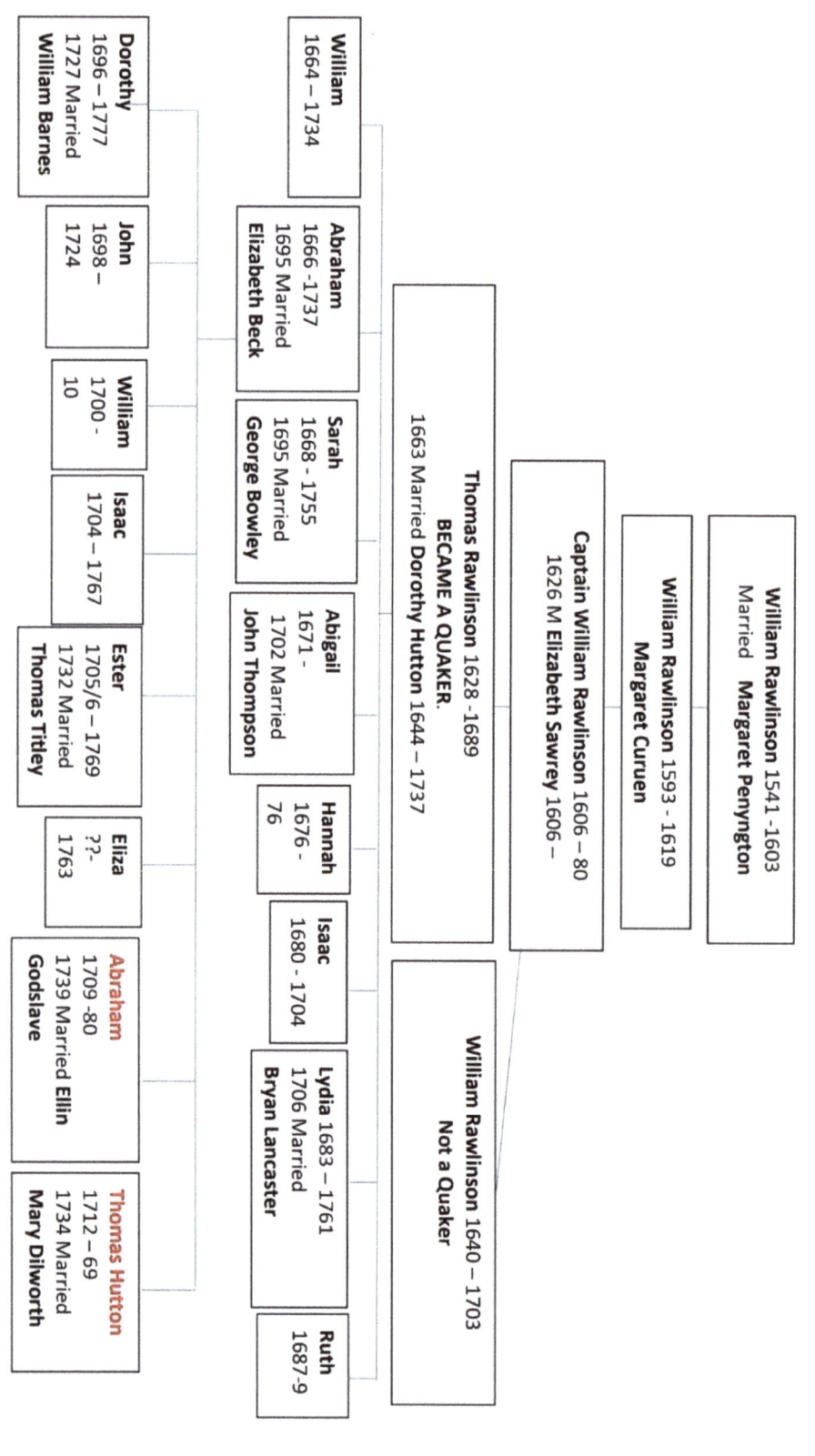

THE RAWLINSONS

The Lancaster Rawlinson families originated in the Hawkshead area of Lancashire. They are descendants of the Rawlinsons of Low Graythwaite & Rusland Halls. Generations of Rawlinsons can be traced back via William 1541 – 1603 and his wife Margaret Pennington to Walter and Henry Rawlinson who fought for Henry V at Agincourt in 1415. They were related to Thomas Rawlinson, the last Abbot of Furness Abbey, which was disestablished and destroyed on the order of Henry VIII in 1537.

William and Margaret's eldest son William, a Parliamentarian in the Civil War, and his wife Elizabeth were not at all content when their eldest son Thomas Rawlinson 1628 -1689 became a first-generation Quaker in 1652. Thomas was banished from the family home.

He became one of the early Quaker missionaries known as the Valiant Sixty. Like other Quakers he suffered periods of imprisonment. In 1656, he was in Exeter prison, sharing a room with James Naylor, a prominent Quaker preacher. In 1657, he was one of the Quakers who accompanied George Fox in Scotland, in the South and South-West of England, and then on to London, where he was present and reported on meetings Fox had with Oliver Cromwell.

In the 1660s, Thomas helped to manage the business affairs of some of the children of Margaret & Judge Fell of Swarthmoor Hall. In 1680, the Fells rented a forge in the Furness area of Lancashire to him.

On 15 July (Quaker 5th month) 1663, Thomas married Dorothy Hutton of Rampside in a Quaker ceremony at a house at Gleaston in the Furness area of Lancashire. This is where the name Hutton in her descendants' names comes from.

The Lancaster Rawlinsons who are the subject of this research are Thomas and Dorothy's grandchildren born to Thomas' second son Abraham and his wife Elizabeth Beck.

It is not clear when Abraham, their eldest son, established an ironworks in Caton just north of Lancaster. Records suggest that a forge in Caton was well established by 1727 and that Myles Birkett, another Lancaster Quaker, was in partnership with Abraham in this venture.

The Rawlinsons were the chief ironmasters in the Backbarrow Company. They supplied a commodity which was not only exported but which was very useful in fitting out the ships being built in Lancaster for the developing markets between Lancaster and the West Indies and ships engaging in the enslaving industry. It is possible that the forge could have made the manacles for the Lancaster slaving ships but their principal products were dog grates for fireplaces.

Thomas Hutton Rawlinson, Abraham's brother, moved to Lancaster and the two brothers became partners in many business ventures. For example, together with Myles Birkett they were active Trustees of the Turnpike Road being built to connect the West and East of the North of England. Westmorland Quaker Alexander Fothergill, the Chief Surveyor, wrote of their involvement between 1745 and 1758 in his diary.

This research will show that the Rawlinson brothers and their children engaged in trafficking enslaved people and owned enslaved Africans on plantations. They and their sons trafficked at least 2,106 enslaved people from Africa to Barbados, Jamaica and Carolina between 1748 and 1776 and fitted out enslaving ships. They owned between them and their extended families 10 plantations. Two family members were compensated in 1836 following emancipation. However the enslaved were then put into 6 year indentureships on their plantations. In Quaker terms all were 'unchristian' actions.

The history of this family's involvement has been followed through in some cases beyond their either being disowned or choosing to leave the Religious Society of Friends. This clearly shows how the money made by them from their involvement in the enslaving industry enhanced their social standing, enabled their sons and grandsons to be well educated, was used to build significant homes, was invested in infrastructure projects and enabled them to establish welfare projects.

Table 9.2 Abraham Rawlinson of Caton's descendants

Abraham Rawlinson
1709 – 80
1739 Married Ellin Godsalve

- **Abigail** 1740 – Married 1791 **William Lindow** 1721-86
- **Henry** 1743 – 86 Married 1765 **Martha Tyzack** 1743 –
  - **Abraham Tyzack** 1777 - 1848
  - **Henry Lindow** 1777 – 1848 Married 1819 **Charlotte Elizabeth Barnard**
- **John** 1744 – 81 Married 1772 **Jane Hodgson** 1745 – 1832
  - **Ann** 1775 - 1832
  - **Abraham** 1776 - 77
  - **Abraham** 1789 - 1829 Married 1814 **Emma Chapman**
  - **John Samuel** 1794 –
- **Ellin** 1745 - 47
- **Dorothy** 1746 - 68
- **William** 1748 - 1811 Married 1781 **Sarah Drury**
- **Thomas** 1749 -49
- **Thomas** 1751 – 1802 Married 1784 **Sarah Cowell**
  - **Mary Toft** 1783 - 4
  - **Sarah Louisa** 1785 - 1851
  - **Ellin Maria** 1789 - 1794
- **Ellin** 1753 – 1816?
- **Abraham Beck** 1754
- **Samuel** 1757 – Married 1810 **Sarah Chorley** 1762 - 90
  - Married 1782

Abraham Rawlinson 1709-80 and his sons Henry 1743 – 1783; John 1744 -81; William 1748 - 1811; Thomas 1751 - 1802 & Samuel 1757 -1810

Abraham Rawlinson of Grassyard Hall painted by George Romney is owned by Lancaster City Museum Service.

Abraham Rawlinson was the sixth child of Abraham and Elizabeth Beck, Quakers of Swarthmoor Monthly Meeting. He was born in Low Graythwaite Hall near Hawkshead, the family home of the Rawlinsons since at least 1540. His father, an iron master, set up a forge in Caton in about 1727.

When looking at the business activities of the Rawlinson family, it is nearly impossible to separate the actions of Abraham and his sons from those of his brother Thomas Hutton and his sons. They were all intricately involved in partnerships with each other and others. The brothers together owned colonial and enslaving ships sailing out of Lancaster and the sugar plantation Goyave in Grenada in the mid-1760s.

In 1736, Abraham, aged 27, was sent to the West Indies to act as a Factor for the family company in Barbados. He thus gained valuable experience in the West Indies Trade. In 1737 Benjamin Satterthwaite was sent out to be his assistant. It was in that year that his father Abraham died. Abraham junior does not appear to return to Lancaster until 1739 but then returns to Barbados in 1740 for a second period. His brother Thomas Hutton took over in the intervening period. During this time, they were shipping cotton back to Lancaster for sale to the cotton mill of Escricke in Bolton.[1]

On 3rd August 1739, Abraham and Ellin Godsalve took each other in marriage at Lancaster Meeting House.[2] The Minute Book of the Preparative Meeting dated 2nd of 11th month 1739 records that Abraham gave a sum of money to the meeting on his marriage but does not identify how much. [3]

They had eleven children:
Abigail 1740, who took William Lindow as her husband 9th December 1771; Henry 1743, whose story follows; John 1744, whose story follows; Ellin 1745, who died in 1747; Dorothy 1746; William 1748; Thomas 1749, who died that year; Thomas 1750 whose story follows; Ellin 1753; Abraham Beck 1754 and Samuel 1757 who married Sarah Chorley.[4]

This portrait of Ellin Rawlinson is by an unknown artist commissioned by her daughter Abigail, owned by Lancaster City Museum Service.

In 1750, on the death of his mother, Abraham and Ellin moved out of their first home on Castle Hill Lancaster to live at Grassyard Hall Caton. It was built around a dwelling first established in 1330 and now called Grassgarth Hall.

Abraham owned and part-owned several ships: in 1746, *Ellen & Jane,* and in 1773, *Lively* registered in Jamaica with his son Henry and nephew Abraham Rawlinson.[5]

The Voyages Database records that Abraham Rawlinson owned a tenth share in the enslaving ship *Clayton* built in London on the Thames that sailed out of Liverpool. It made three voyages from Liverpool to Bonny, Nigeria: in 1748, embarking 272 enslaved, of whom 223 were disembarked in Kingston; in 1750, trafficking 380 enslaved, of whom 312 were disembarked in Barbados; and in 1752, setting out to traffic 310 enslaved, after which the Portuguese captured it. Thus, 962 enslaved were trafficked, of whom 117 died during the middle passages. This ship, on its first voyage, had 16 guns and 4 guns on the subsequent voyages. There is no evidence in the Monthly Meeting archive of Abraham being challenged about having these 'instruments of war' on a ship in which he owned shares. Abraham's fellow investors are not Lancaster Quakers. One was William Gregson, the most prolific of the Liverpool Slave Traders. How Abraham became involved with him is not clear.[6]

We have seen in William Dillworth's story that in 1752 the ship *Providence* left Barbados for South Carolina with 'twenty new negros'. That ship was part-owned by Abraham and Thomas Hutton Rawlinson, Thomas and William Dillworth, John Rowlandson and Captain Jonathan Nicholson. A Lancaster partnership that included non-Quakers as well as Quakers.

Imagined portrait of John Chance by Lela Harris 2022 displayed in the Judges Lodgings Museum Lancaster. Facing the Past Project.

Abraham and Thomas Hutton were also in partnership with William Lindow, Abraham's non-Quaker son-in-law, who married Abigail, Abraham's eldest child, in 1771 at St Mary's church. Lindow was captain of some of the Rawlinson ships and a Factor for them. He had 1 Queen's Square Lancaster designed, built and furnished by Robert Gillow for his bride. There, they had a black servant, John Chance, who was baptised at St Mary's on 12th September 1777 and is described in the record as 'a black man aged 22 years and upwards in the service of Mr Lindow.'[7]

Together, from about 1773, the partnership owned the ships *Lindow* and *Kerie*, the latter ship described in 1763 as a prize from the French in the London Certificate of Freedom.[8] Clearly, they engaged in privateering.

MM Schofield, in his paper 'Lancashire Colonial Exports', notes that the Rawlinson brothers of Lancaster in 1785 exported to the West Indies:

'Quantities of foodstuffs, mostly from Ireland, but including more expensive foods from Lancashire; candles in great quantities and soap; textiles of all sorts; furniture from many other Lancaster firms as well as the Gillows; ironmongery; pottery and glassware; 'curled hair' (for upholstery?); hats, caps and shoes; saddlery, stationery; and sailcloth and twine. Some of these were from Lancaster firms, others from all over the county. From Lonsdale north of the Sands, there were goods from Broughton, Ulverston, Penny Bridge and Flookborough. Near Lancaster, there were suppliers of goods in Grange, Silverdale, Ellel, Galgate, Catterall, Myerscough and Wyresdale. In South Lancashire, goods came from Preston, Walton, Leyland, Clayton Green, Bolton, Wigan, Warrington and, of course, from Manchester textiles.'[9]

Rawlinson 'Voyage Book No. 3' held in Lancaster Library also gives information about British manufactured goods exported. 'Osnaburghs', a coarse plain weave fabric originally woven in flax but also in jute, were bought from John Platt of Wigan and from William Pollard and Henry Critchley, both of Leyland. This was in a voyage list for September 1787 and there were repeat orders from the Leyland men in 1789 and 1790. In a list for March 1788 'Osnaburghs' were brought from James Smith of Glasgow and in June 1790 'Scotch Osnaburghs' were brought through a Lancaster merchant from Alexander Morrison of Dundee with repeat orders through to 1795. It is suggested that the Rawlinson brothers bought more cloth to export than any other manufactured goods. [10]

Clearly, the brothers were scouring Lancashire and further afield for non-perishable goods of value which could be traded in the West Indies. In addition, they searched in Ireland:

'Other foodstuffs were a regular part of exports, particularly to the West Indies. Most of the salt beef, pork and butter was shipped at Irish ports, particularly from Cork, Waterford and Belfast.' [11]

Abraham, with his brother Thomas Hutton and William Lindow each had a third share in the sugar plantation Goyave in Grenada. It is believed that William Lindow, who spent a good deal of his time out there as a Factor, was responsible for the initial investment and invited the Rawlinson brothers to join him. [12]

In 1779, Abraham and his son Thomas, along with Abraham's nephews Abraham and John, were visited by appointed Lancaster Quaker Monthly Meeting Elders. The Monthly Meeting had been discerning from April of that year what action they might take in relation to the family having an armed ship with a Letter of Marque engaged in privateering. This was against the Quaker Testimony to Peace.

Both Abraham and Thomas apologised to the Meeting and were felt not to have profited from this act of privateering so no further action was taken. [13]

Abraham died the following year in 1780 and is buried in the grounds of Lancaster Meeting House.

In his Will 4th November 1780, he left property to his sons apart from William and Samuel Rawlinson, to whom he left money.

Henry Rawlinson 1743 – 1786

Henry, Abraham's eldest son, also worked as a West India Merchant, thus supporting the enslaving industry. He formed the company Rawlinson & Chorley with John Chorley, a Liverpool Quaker,[14,] who became his cousin by his marriage to Sara Rawlinson, daughter of Thomas Hutton Rawlinson.

In 1765 Henry and Martha Tyzack took each other in marriage at Newcastle Friend's Meeting House. They had ten children together, eight girls of whom three died in infancy. The births of these girls between 1766 and 1776 are all recorded in the Lancaster Monthly Meeting register. [15]

Henry moved his business operations to Liverpool and employed a Factor, Richard Heatherington, to work for him on the island of Tortola. The Rawlinson Chorley partnership took apprentices, including John Bolton from Ulverston, who they sent to the Caribbean between 1773 and 1783. He returned a wealthy man and one of the most prolific of the Liverpool enslaving traders and plantation owners.

That Henry, his wife and his family had moved to Liverpool is recorded in the Lancaster Preparative Meeting minutes of the 4th of the 10 month of 1772. The meeting is concerned that no certificate of transfer has been applied for.[16] This was important as meetings took a good deal of responsibility for families who were members of their meeting. This was reported to the Monthly Meeting.

Lancaster Quaker Monthly Meeting Minutes on the 6th of the 10th month of 1772 recorded that Henry Rawlinson and family had removed to Hardshaw East but that no certificate of removal had been applied for. William Dillworth, Joshua Whalley and William Jepson were appointed to prepare one. [17]

The Trans-Atlantic Slave Trade Voyages Database shows the voyage of *Molly* sailing from Liverpool to Iles de Los 1776, owned by John Chorley, Abraham Rawlinson Jr., Henry Rawlinson and Moses Benson. 328 enslaved boarded of whom 300 disembarked in Jamacia. Thus, 28 died at sea. [18]

In 1776, with his cousins Abraham and John Chorley, Henry bought the Maran Estate on Grenada in the district of St Marks. [19] This plantation and Goyave, are shown on the UCL Legacies of British Slavery Database to have between 259 and 1,482 enslaved people working on them during the period of their ownership.

Henry's twin sons Abraham Tyzack and Henry Lindow were born on 17 July 1777 in Liverpool and registered in the Quaker birth records of Hardshaw East Quaker Monthly Meeting that year. [20]

However, Henry and Martha were baptised in the Anglican church as adults on 10th September 1780. Henry is described in the St Ann of Richmond Church record as 'of riper years' a Merchant living in Clayton Square, Liverpool. [21]

A minute written after Henry's death makes it clear that both Henry and Martha were disowned by Hardshaw East Monthly Meeting on the 19th day of the 10th Month of 1779. [22] It is not clear why they were disowned but it is the same year and time of year that Henry's father, brother Thomas and cousins Abraham and John were visited for privateering, both Abraham and John being disowned.

Henry's disownment made the way clear for him to stand as the MP for Liverpool in 1780, as in 1780 Quakers were still barred from standing for Parliament. Henry was the MP for Liverpool between 1780 and 1784. He did not stand in the election of 1784.

During the 1780s, the Rawlinson partnerships of Rawlinson & Chorley and Rawlinson, Chorley & Grierson were the major importers of West Indian cotton into Liverpool.[23] Much would have been sold on to Manchester, by now known as Cottonopolis, but some would probably have been sold to The Cark Cotton Mill of Thackray, Stockdale and Co in Lancaster.

All seven of his surviving children were baptised in the same church in Everton on 25th January 1781, the oldest being 15 and the youngest, the twins 3.5 years. [24] They lived at Grassyard Hall in Caton which he inherited on his father's death in 1780.

Henry died in 1786 aged just 43 and was buried at St John's Church Lancaster. Following his death, the Hardshaw Monthly Meeting took steps to remove any confusion about the position of Henry & Martha's children in relation to Friends and the responsibility of Friends towards them as this minute records.

Hardshaw East Monthly Meeting 20th of 3rd month 1787 Minute 14

'This meeting having taken into consideration the situation of the children of Martha Rawlinson and her late husband Henry Rawlinson of Liverpool deceased, namely, Maria, Ellen, Elizabeth, Martha, Abraham and Henry, all born before their parents were disowned by this Meeting 19th of 10th Mo 1779. Soon after, them and their children declined their attendance at our religious Meetings; they had the ceremony called Water Baptisms performed upon them by a Priest belonging to the Church of England and have since continued to be Members of that Religious Society also by a letter from their Mother Martha Rawlinson to Wm Rathbone, dated 8th of this M^o on behalf of the said children 'We are informed they have no other intention but to continue Members of said Society. It is therefore concluded by this Meeting that the aforesaid children are no longer to be considered of our religious society… A copy of this Minute to be published in the Preparative Meeting of Liverpool and sent to Martha Rawlinson the elder and her Children.'

Henry Rawlinson's twin sons

The lives of Henry's sons show clearly how money that accrued from the profits of the enslaving industry to the family was used to improve their social standing and that of subsequent generations.

Abraham Tyzack Rawlinson 1777- 1848

Abraham, the elder of the twins by 20 minutes, was educated at Rugby School and Christ Church Oxford. He became a broker. He married Eliza Eudocia Albinia Creswicke on 18 August 1800 in St. George's Hanover Obituary Square, London.[25] Eliza was born in Morton in Marsh, Oxfordshire. Abraham inherited Grassyard Hall on his mother's death in 1807, selling it to buy Chadlington Hall in Oxfordshire. Abraham and Eliza had 8 children, their eldest son becoming Sir Henry Creswick Rawlinson, 1st Baronet, who, according to the Times, was a brilliant Oriental scholar and most distinguished Anglo-Indian statesman. Abraham Tyzack was buried in Oxfordshire in 1848.

Henry Lindow Rawlinson 1777 – 1848

Henry's name was changed to Henry Lindow Lindow when, in 1787, aged 10, he inherited the arms of his uncle by marriage William Lindow.[26] On the death of his Aunt Abigail Lindow in 1791 he also inherited William's estate. This estate comprised shares in 3 plantations on Grenada and St Vincent; parcels of land both urban and agricultural on other islands and in several other islands including Grenada; the Grenadines, St Vincent; Dominica and Tortola. In 1786, he also inherited the estate Maran owned by his father in Grenada.

Henry, a very wealthy young man, was like his twin brother educated at Rugby and Christ Church Oxford. In August 1819 he married Charlotte Elizabeth Barnard of Wethersfield, Suffolk.

He was compensated in 1833 for enslaved people he still owned on the two plantations in St Vincent, the Fountain Estate, where he owned 99 -100 enslaved and for the Kearton Estate, where he owned 14 enslaved. The compensation figures he was awarded were £3,127.11sh. 8d for Fountain and for Kearton £178.18sh. 4d. [27] (In 2024, this represents £330,955).

He died a wealthy man in 1848 in Lower Slaughter, Gloucestershire. Probate was granted in 1849. [28]

John Rawlinson 1744 -1781

Abraham and Ellin's third child, John, owned a share in an enslaving ship, *Sarah*, with his partner and non-Quaker brother-in-law William Lindow.[29] In 1773, it transported 148 enslaved from the Sierra Leone Estuary to Grenada. Only 131 disembarked.

On 29 October 1772, John and Jane Hodgson took each other in marriage in the Friends Meeting House in Newcastle at their weekday meeting. They had two children. Ann was born in 1775 and died unmarried 24th April 1832, just 8 days after her mother in Benwell Northumberland. Abraham, born in 1776, died the next year. [30]

Two John Rawlinsons are listed as Additional Port Commissioners of Lancaster by Melinda Elder. She states 'they had singular Investments in slaving during their period in office, one in 1770 - 73, the other in 1773 – 1776'.[31] Which is Abraham's son and which is Thomas Hutton's son is not clear, but this John may have served from 1773 as that is the period when his partner William Lindow was also a Port Commissioner.

John died on 19 July 1781 aged just 37 and was buried in Lancaster Friends Meeting Ground. The Monthly Meeting Clerk in 1781 was William Dillworth as we have seen another merchant involved in the enslaving industry.

In his Will John left his money to family members, including his sisters and to his brother-in-law William Lindow. William Lindow also inherited the apartments John owned on the Quay. [32] It is not clear what happened to John's part share in the plantation which in 1780 he inherited from his father.

William Rawlinson 1748 - 1811 & Samuel Rawlinson 1757 – 1810

In 1766, William, Abraham and Ellin's sixth child was apprenticed to his cousin by marriage, Isaac Ford, a Quaker Check Manufacturer in Manchester.[33]

Isaac Ford's company, along with a core of other Manchester cotton manufacturers, produced 'coarse checks' (cloth or fabric with a pattern of crossed lines) and silk handkerchiefs. The industry reportedly earned Manchester up to £200,000 per annum, equivalent to £28m today. It was mostly cloth that was traded for captured Africans, but it was also sold to the plantations.

Once his apprenticeship was completed William set up his own manufacturing operation, eventually going into partnership with his youngest brother Samuel and Christian Godfrey Alberti. It is highly likely that William and Samuel used their Quaker contacts in Lancaster to purchase the raw materials and then supplied them with this cloth to export. However, when the American War of Independence interrupted this flow of goods in 1775, William and Samuel turned their attention to trading with Europe. [34]

In 1781, William married Sarah Drury. He married out. He does not appear to have been disowned for this action by the Lancaster Quaker Monthly Meeting nor to have moved his membership to a Manchester Quaker Meeting. William bought Ancots Hall Manchester. When doing so he is described as a wealthy Manchester Manufacturer.

In 1782, Samuel married Sarah Chorley, part of the Quaker Chorley family in Staffordshire. [35]

In 1795, the partnership with Alberti was dissolved.[36]

These brothers, although not directly involved in trafficking or owning enslaved Africans, inherited money accrued by their father from trafficking and owning enslaved Africans. They made a good living out of manufacturing goods using material produced by the enslaved and then selling those goods back to the West Indies. They were very clearly engaged in the enslaving industry.

Thomas Rawlinson 1751 – 1802

Thomas, the eighth child of Abraham and Elling, was named by his parents after a brother born in 1749 who died that year. He entered the family business and became involved in the ownership of enslaved people.

As we have already seen, in 1779, Thomas and his father Abraham were visited by the Monthly Meeting Elders for profiteering. Both apologised but, as it was believed that they did not profit, they were not disowned. [37]

In 1784, Thomas and Sarah Cowell, daughter of a Leeds Quaker Merchant, took each other in marriage in Bradford Meeting House. They had eight children: Hannah Garbutt, 1785; Ellin, 1786; Abigail Dorothea, 1787; Abraham, 1789; William, 1790; Thomas, 1791; Sarah, 1792; and John Samuel, 1794. Lydia Rawlinson, the unmarried daughter of Thomas Hutton Rawlinson and Thomas's cousin, attended the births of Sarah's first four children. [38]

For her last four confinements Sarah had the attendance of a Surgeon, a sign of Thomas' growing wealth.

Thomas part-owned the *Abbey,* which conveyed 180 'new Negros' between St. Vincent and Tobago in 1786. He was involved in the secondary trafficking of the enslaved. [39]

The year is of interest as it is the year after the London Yearly Meeting request of 1784 repeated in 1785 that inquiries should be made into Friends involved in the Transatlantic Slave Trade and the outcome reported to the Yearly Meeting. In the second month of 1785, the Lancaster Monthly Meeting Minutes reported that:

'… none concerned that we know of in the importation of them (negros) from Africa…' [40]

A true statement at the time to an inquiry that only looked at one aspect of the enslaving industry, trafficking, rather than wider aspects in which some Lancaster Quaker Merchants were still involved, such as plantation ownership. It was in November 1780 that Thomas had inherited shares from his father in the Goyave plantation in Grenada and, with his partner, Anglican Thomas Bond, set about planning their entry into further plantation ownership.

On 24 February 1792, Quaker James Howarth wrote to John Field, Quaker Grocer of Lancaster, Cashier and Elder for Lancaster Monthly Meeting, about an annuity left in the Will of Robert Waterhouse to his parents that was not being paid. In the letter, he added:

Lydia Rawlinson. Unknown artist on display in the Judges Lodgings Museum Lancaster

'Whilst I am writing to you. I must mention another matter. A Friend from the county of York, being lately in this neighbourhood, mentioned to several of us that a member of your Monthly Meeting had Plantations in the West Indies with slaves upon them and seemed under great concern about it, to which we were strangers and could not resolve him. Still, he seemed desirous that some of us of this county would enquire into it and was surprised that a thing of this magnitude should remain in our Society. So, I thought it not improper just to hint to thee not with a view to dictate to you your duty but to convey the Friend's concern, for if such a thing do *(sic)* exist, I can scarcely doubt that you have attended to it, in some respect.' [41]

This could only refer to Thomas Rawlinson. The matter of the annuity seems to have been acted on. In the subsequent correspondence, there is no reference to the Meeting taking up with Thomas Rawlinson his ownership of enslaved people nor in the minute book of that year or subsequent years of this matter being placed before the Preparative Meeting; Monthly Meeting or Quarterly Meeting of Ministers and Elders.

Thomas was clearly making a significant profit from this activity as in July 1792 he had sufficient disposable income to subscribe £5,000 (approximately £628,029 in 2024) to the building of the Lancaster Canal, as the Subscribers Notebook, owned by Lancaster Museum Service, shows.

Lancaster Quaker Meeting seems to have had other concerns in relation to Thomas as the 1793 minutes of Lancaster Preparative Meeting 3rd day of 2nd-month record:

'Robert Routh informed this meeting that Overseers had had an opportunity with Thomas Rawlinson, who was balloted to serve in the Militia, and they were informed by him that a substitute had been hired and that one of his servants had paid the expenses incurred thereon, which our representations are required to lay before Monthly Meeting.' [42]

As we have seen with James Nottage, this was a common way for those with money to avoid either serving in the Militia or being imprisoned. Quakers, however, were expected to refuse this option and accept being sent to prison.

In the 3rd month of 1793 his name is again recorded in the Preparative Meeting minutes for a different concern:

'Thomas Rawlinson, a member of this meeting, has so far deviated from our Christian Testimony against war and fighting as to put a number of guns on his vessel of which he is part owner and intends to proceed with her on her voyage, which our representatives are desired to lay before Monthly Meeting.'

Monthly Meeting appointed John Field and Charles Parker to visit him. They reported in the 5th month of 1793, and the minute reads:

'The Thomas Rawlinson case having come solidly under the consideration of this meeting; his conduct appears to be highly inconsistent with our profession. It calls for the exercise of the rules of our discipline notwithstanding from a desire to convince him of his errors.'

In the 9th month, the minute reads:
'We are informed that if asked to serve again he would deal with the matter within Friends rules – satisfactory to the meeting.' [43]

No mention seems to have been made in this visit of the guns on his ship nor of the letter sent to John Field about Thomas's ownership of enslaved people. If these matters were discussed with him, there is no record in the minutes of the Preparative, Monthly or Quarterly Meetings.

In the 11th month of 1794 Thomas is identified as the next Friend to accompany Traveling Friends by the Preparative Meeting.

Furthermore, in 1796, Thomas Rawlinson and his partner Anglican Thomas Bond from Over Kellett borrowed £10,000 from the British government under the Grenada and St Vincent loans scheme (the equivalent of £947,859 in 2024) to buy four further plantations! A single repayment of £3,333 6s 8d was recorded in January 1799. The rest of the loan/mortgage appears eventually to have been repaid. [44]

He had shares in the Bond plantation named Broom Hall in Demerara, British Guiana, growing sugar where the conditions of those enslaved were said to be beyond cruel and appalling. They were absentee landlords. [45]

Thomas lived for some time in Liverpool but died falling off his horse between Lancaster and Yealand and was buried in Yealand Friends Burial Ground in 1802. Thus, he did not live to read the account by George Pickard MD of the way the enslaved were treated on his Lancaster plantation.

Thomas' Will dated 14th October 1802 instructed his trustees (John Bond, John Proctor and William Sanderson, all Merchants of Lancaster) on his death to sell his land at Yealand Conyers in the county of Lancaster and at Burton-in-Kendal in the county of Westmoreland. His estates and shares in estates in St Vincent and Grenada and all the estates conveyed to him by way of mortgage in St Vincent, Grenada, Berbice and Demerara, were left for the benefit of his children, to share and share alike, with the proviso that his eldest son Abraham Rawlinson, banker, should receive £1,000 more than any other of his children. [46]

The selling of these plantations resulted in the enslaved on them either being transferred to the new owner or sold separately. Separately selling the enslaved meant that families were split up, including children from their mothers. Some were transported miles from where they had been placed when they arrived from Africa or where they had been born into enslavement. No thought was given to their family connections. On the inventories, they appear as chattels.

Footnote
In 1800 the ship *Fraternite* was taken 'as a prize' from the French by the Rawlinsons. It held 195 enslaved, of whom 14 died during the middle passage. Thomas Rawlinson had a part share in this ship.[81]

Abraham Rawlinson 1789 – 1829

Thomas Rawlinson's eldest son and co-heir became a banker, a partner in Gurneys, Birkbeck & Rawlinson, a Quaker Bank in Fakenham Norfolk. He became the managing partner in 1817.

Abraham Rawlinson was disowned by the Monthly Meeting on 28 March 1811 '… declined to attend and so forfeits his birthright to membership'.[47]

On 26 April 1814, he married Emma Chapman in Wanstead, Essex. They had two sons, Thomas (1816) and William Chapman (1818).[48]

His cousin Ann Ford had married Robert Barclay, Banker of Lombard Street, in 1783 and in 1814 Elizabeth Gurney, daughter of Abraham's partner, married their son Robert Barclay. These two banking companies, along with Backhouse and Co, Quaker Bankers in Darlington, came together on 30th March 1896 to form Barclays Bank, the founding of Barclays Bank Ltd. [49]

Abraham was buried at Lancaster Priory on 20 August 1829, aged 40. [50] His Will makes no mention of plantations and he died prior to emancipation. However, Booker's account books of the period suggest that Thomas Rawlinson's heirs remained in part ownership with Thomas Bond of the Broom Hall Plantation in what is now Guyana in the 1820s. The UCL Legacies of Slavery Database shows Abraham Rawlinson and heirs being in ownership from 1817 – 1834. In 1835, the owners of Broom Hall received compensation, the equivalent in 2024 to £1,051,697, for the freeing of their 191 enslaved people. [51]

Table 9.3 Thomas Hutton Rawlinson's descendants

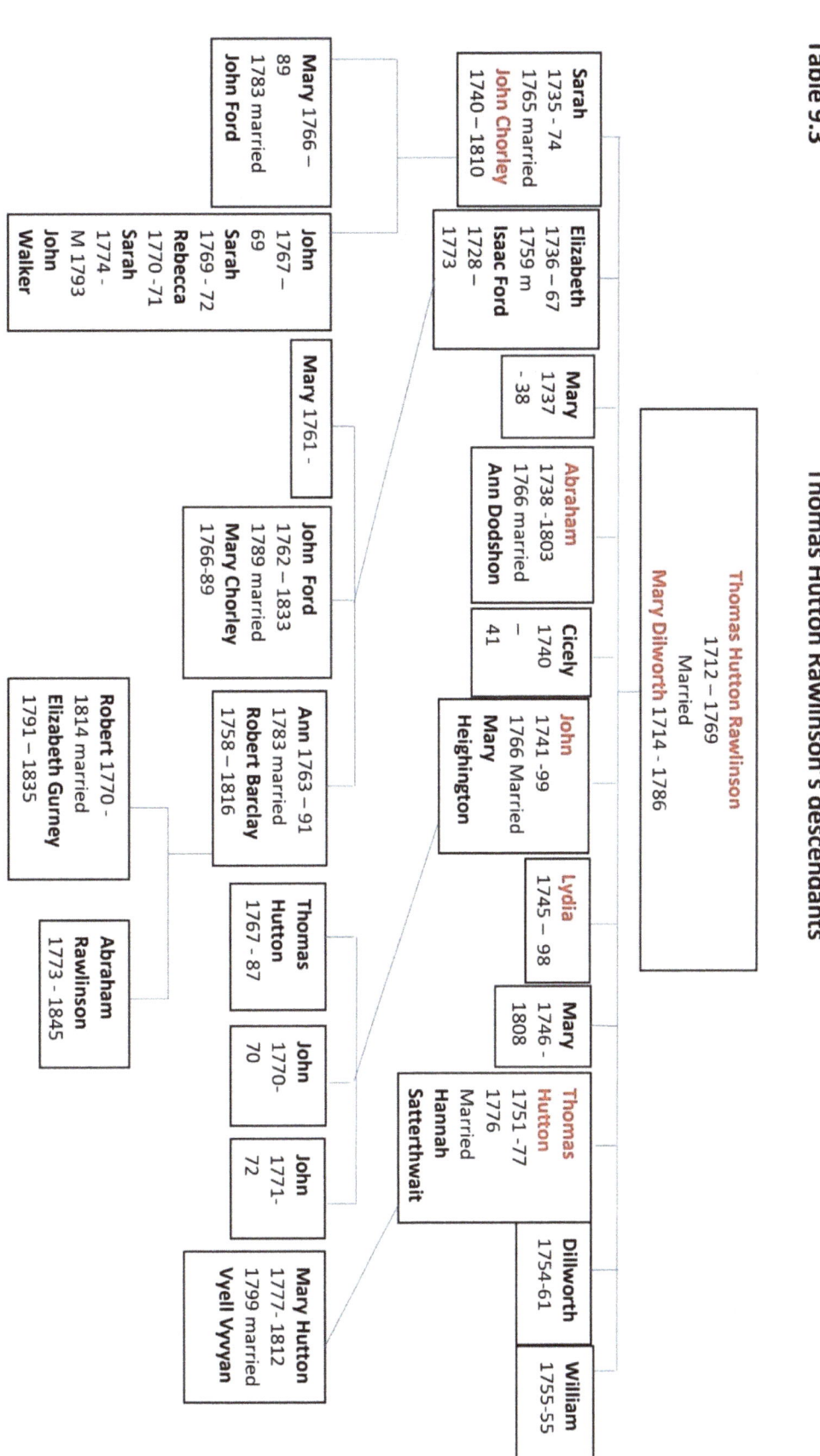

Thomas Hutton Rawlinson 1712 – 69 and his sons Abraham 1738 – 1803; John 1741 – 99 and Thomas Hutton 1751 - 1777

Portrait of Thomas Hutton Rawlinson on display in the Maritime Museum Lancaster painted by George Romney

Born into a Quaker Family on 02 May 1712, Thomas Hutton (senior) was the youngest of the ten children of Abraham Rawlinson, the iron master of Furness and Caton. He was named Hutton after his maternal grandmother Dorothy. [52]

Thomas Hutton started as a sea captain prior to establishing himself as a merchant in Lancaster. He captained the colonial trading ship *Industry* in 1735. This ship, owned by the Dillworth, Townson & Rawlinson merchants, made repeated voyages to Barbados during the 1730s. [53]

On 04 December 1734, Thomas Hutton Rawlinson and Mary Dillworth took each other in marriage at Lancaster Meeting House further cementing the business partnership. They had eleven children.[54]

His imports included mahogany for Robert Gillow whose furniture was also exported to the West Indies by this Lancaster partnership.

With other members of the family and Lancaster merchants, he was the owner or part owner of several ships used for colonial trading, including the *Molly* (1743), *Ellen* (1746), *Jane* (1746), *Recovery* (1746), *Industry* (1744-1752) and the enslaving ships *Phoenix* (1744) which embarked 148 enslaved in Benin and trafficked them to the Caribbean with 17 dying at sea and *Wynstay* (1744) which embarked 102 enslaved in Bonny trafficking them to the Caribbean, 10 dying at sea.[55]

Portrait of Mary Rawlinson on display in the Judges Lodgings Museum Lancaster painted by George Romney

His interests, with his eldest son Abraham, included shipping the enslaved between the islands of the West Indies. We have already seen that a ship, *Providence* part owned by Thomas Hutton and Abraham with the Dillworth brothers, left Barbados in 1752 bound for South Carolina carrying '20 New Negros'. Another Rawlinson ship left Grenada for Cape Fear with a cargo of coarse linen and 10 enslaved people.

Between 1752 and 1762, more Rawlinson vessels were registered with the Lancaster Port authorities than those of other Lancaster merchants. In 1756, the Rawlinson families owned at least eight of the seventeen vessels returning from the West Indies and the mainland of America. [56]

In 1756, his son Abraham Junior took over the company and consolidated the Lancaster interests in the enslavement industry in a new company, 'Abraham Rawlinson Junior Company & Co,'. It has not been possible to ascertain why Thomas Hutton, a relatively young man of 44 years, was content to take a back seat. What is significant about this development is that Abraham's mother and unmarried sister Lydia were each given a sixth share in the new company. [57]

The Rawlinson family was directly involved in Liverpool partnerships including that of Rawlinson & Chorley based in Old Hall St. This association was made even stronger by the marriage in 1765 of Thomas Hutton Rawlinson's eldest daughter Sarah to John, the son of his partner Alexander Chorley and his wife Rebecca, of Rainhill. [58]

Melinda Elder writes that 'There are no surviving naval office shipping lists for the years 1767 – 1784, the period when seventeen or more Lancaster slavers sailed from Africa for Grenada. However, the island's rapid development at this time supports this supposition…'. Indeed, Lancaster's most prominent West Indian merchants, Thomas Hutton and Abraham Rawlinson, and later their sons, became the owners of the Goyave Sugar Plantation in Grenada from the mid-1760s.' [59]

As we have seen their ownership of a third part each resulted from their involvement with William Lindow. This was despite London Yearly Meeting in 1758 minuting that Friends should avoid profits from dealing in negros and in 1761 recommending that any Quakers found to have slaves should be disowned by their religious community.

Thomas Hutton died on the 16th day of the 7th month of 1769 and is buried in the Lancaster Meeting burial ground.[60]

In his Will he made an endowment to Lancaster Friends' School of £200 (the equivalent of £35,576 in 2024) to be held in Trust and invested in land or government securities. The interest that accrued was to be used to pay a schoolmaster to teach Friends' children and to buy educational books for poor Friends' children. [61] He insisted that his sons were Trustees. This fund was eventually handed to other charitable Education funds in 1915 by the Lancaster Monthly Meeting with the agreement of the Charity Commission.

On his death, his wife Mary received £5,000 (the equivalent in 2024 of £764,402) and her substantial house.

In July 1772 she took delivery of the ornate bookcase she had commissioned to be made by Robert Gillow's company. It was principally made by Thomas & John Dowbiggin. It is the most fully provenanced Gillow piece of furniture in existence and a detailed estimate for its manufacture is held in the Gillow Archive in Westminster City Library. It cost £17.17sh.0d. (£2,562 in 2024) and is currently in the Judges Lodgings Museum in Lancaster.

Mary continued to receive the income from her one-sixth share in the Rawlinson company till her death in 1786.

Abraham Rawlinson Junior 1738 – 1803

Abraham, Thomas Hutton and Mary's eldest son, entered the family West Indies trading business taking over the role occupied by his father as head of the company in 1756.

It is the surviving account book in the Lancaster Reference Library which shows that in creating the new company, Abraham Rawlinson Junior & Co., Abraham gave his mother and sister Lydia each a sixth share. This was a bold step at that time although women from the gentry and nobility were involved in banks, insurance and companies. Two Quaker women were now directly involved in the trafficking and ownership of enslaved people, although possibly silent partners in the company.

The company was heavily involved in the importation of mahogany from Jamaica and was the primary importer for the Lancaster furniture-making Gillow Company. The skills involved in felling mahogany trees are thought to have been taken by the enslaved from West Africa to Jamaica. 90% of the mahogany imported to Britain in this period came from Jamaica. For the enslaved men, women and children who were forced to do this work, life was strenuous. In Jamaica, enslaved Africans worked on and off for three months in gangs of 30 to 40. The men were the principal cutters and haulers while the women worked to drag and clean up the heavy branches that the children then bundled.[62]

The company imported other goods produced by the labour of the enslaved and was involved in trafficking them from Africa. The Trans- Atlantic Slave Trade Voyages Database shows the voyage of the *Molly* to Jamaica from Africa in 1776, owned by John Chorley, Abraham Rawlinson Jr., Henry Rawlinson and Moses Benson, carrying 328 enslaved people from Iles de Los, of whom only 300 were disembarked in Jamaica. [64]

It is said that Abraham was going to settle in Liverpool in 1763 to trade from there but he remained in Lancaster.

On 29 May 1766 he and Ann Dodshon, daughter of Robert Dodshon, a gentleman, and his wife Elizabeth, took each other in marriage in Durham Wallnook Meeting House. It was a double wedding as his younger brother John married Mary Heightington there the same day. [63] Abraham and Ann had no children.

In the 1770s Abraham had Ellel Hall built to a Robert Adams' design. [65] This was a clear example of the profits made from the enslaving industry being put into property in the area around Lancaster.

Abraham Rawlinson Junior Portrait painted by George Romney in 1767 in the Rococo style on display in the Judges Lodgings Museum Lancaster.

Early Friends had Queries produced by the London Yearly Meeting. Queries were sent out and considered by all Monthly Meetings who had to respond in writing about how they investigated the queries, a report on this being sent to the next London Yearly Meeting session. Between 1776 and 1803, Lancaster Monthly Meeting would have had to investigate and report on what they found about Friends not complying with the following Query 11:

'Do you bear a faithful Testimony against bearing arms or paying Trophy money, or being in any way concerned in the militia? In Privateering, Letters of Mark, armed vessels or in dealing in prize goods as such' [66]

In September 1779, Abraham and his brother John with his uncle Abraham senior, cousin Thomas and Samuel Bradford were visited by Lancaster Monthly Meeting Elders. The Monthly Meeting had been discussing this from March of that year when they had been informed that:

'Diverse Friends of this meeting are concerned in an armed vessel furnished with a Letter of Marque under which some of them took the property of others contrary to the right practices of our Redeemer and our ancient church testimony in particular.'

The minute continues:

'The following Friends are appointed to visit them and to report on their service to the next meeting: Samuel Routh, Joshua Whalley, Jonathan Harrison, John Birkbeck with any other Friend or Friends who may be inclined to accompany them in this service.' [67]

The Monthly Meeting left the matter under consideration in June, July and August. The matter was referred to the Quarterly Meeting and London Yearly Meeting. In September, the minute did not name the four men. The meeting was still waiting to hear from them and the decision to give them more time clearly took a great deal of thought given how altered the minute is.

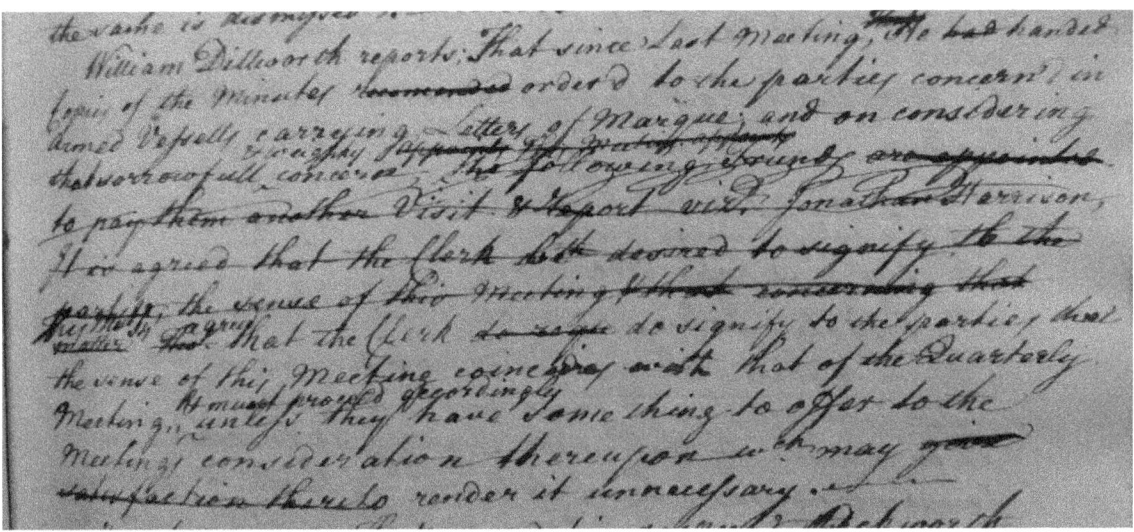

The resulting minute reads:

'William Dillworth reports that since the last meeting, he handed copies of the minutes ordered to the parties concerned in Armed Vessells carrying Letters of Mark, and on considering that sorrowful and weighty concern, they met in a group. That the Clerk do signify to the parties that some of this Meetine (sic) coincided with that of Quarterly Meeting. It must proceed accordingly unless they have something to offer to the Meetings consideration thereupon which may render it unnecessary.'

A decision was made in November 1779. A 'Testimony of Denial' on Abraham Senior and Thomas was suspended as they had not profited from the Letter of Marque. However, Abraham Junior his brother John and Samuel Bradford were to be disowned by a public 'Testimony of Denial' as they had prospered by their Letter of Marque.

The minute reads:
'The matter remaining those concerned in Letters of Marque left to further consideration & nothing being offered by them thereupon at last meeting has come closely under the weighty consideration of this Meeting, And it appears that the case of Abraham Rawlinson, John Rawlinson his brother and Samuel Bradford is different in a considerable degree from the other, by having prospered themselves of the property of another under care of letters of marque contrary to the Righteous

precept of our Saviour. It is the sense of this Meeting that a Testimony be drawn up against such practices and them as concerned therein. The following Friends are appointed to prepare a Testimony accordingly to be produced at the next Meeting visit. Joshua Whalley Saml. Routh, William Jepson, William Dillworth, John Birket, John Routh, Jonathan Whalley, Joshus Robinson & Richd. Margot, who are…'

Abraham did not continue to attend Quaker Meetings as had others for whom a 'Testimony of Denial and Disownment' had been enacted. He was baptised at St Mary's Church four months after his disownment.

'Baptism: 25 Mar 1780 St Mary, Lancaster, Lancashire, England
Abraham Rawlinson, Junr. Esq. –
Abode: Lancr.
Notes: An Adult, formally one of the People called Quakers.
Register: Baptisms 1749 – 1786 Page 141 Entry 4
Source: LDS Film 1526146' [68]

This new religious allegiance enabled him to stand for Parliament. In 1780, Abraham Rawlinson, on declaring himself a parliamentary candidate for Lancaster, was said to be worth 'upwards of £40,000 besides a landed estate, Ellel Hall, and of £500 per annum' [69]. If indeed Abraham was worth £40,000 plus in 1780, (in 2024 that would represent £6,031,363). He served as the Member of Parliament for Lancaster from 1780 to 1790.

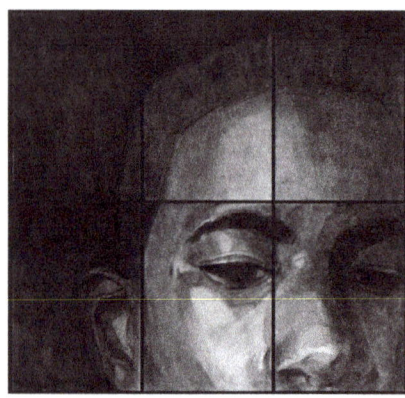

An imagined portrait of Isaac Rawlinson by Lela Harris 2022 displayed in the Judges Lodgings Museum Lancaster, Facing the Past Project.

The record of baptisms at St John's Anglican Church, dated 3rd February 1783, shows that of Isaac Rawlinson a negro adult. It is not clear if Isaac was a free man or still enslaved but, given his name and Abraham Rawlinson's connection to St John's Anglican Church, it is very possible that he was Abraham's servant.

It is interesting that Abraham did not have black servants whilst in membership of the Lancaster Monthly Meeting but, once disowned, probably acquired this servant and possibly the servant called William Dilworth whose baptism was discussed earlier. Maybe his membership of the Religious Society of Friends had some restraining influence on him.

During this period of disownment, he made a gift of the organ to St John's Church. The guidebook says:

'The organ was dedicated on 2 January 1785 as a gift of Abram Rawlinson Esq MP. Rawlinson was a Quaker who was expelled from the Quaker Church for carrying guns on one of his ships. The organ was built in 1784 by Langshaw. The case was made by Gillows.'

It would appear that Abraham felt it better to be known for having guns on his ships rather than for prospering from the taking of the property of another.

In 1788, the Slave Trade Act was passed, limiting the number of enslaved that a ship could carry to 1.67 per ton. This Act had to be renewed annually. Abraham opposed this and the Abolition of the Slave Trade throughout his parliamentary career.

In his letter book in 1792, on the sugar boycott campaign led by abolitionists, he recorded:

'the people in England want to lower the prices of sugar and yet continue presenting petitions from all quarters to Parliament to procure the abolition of the slave trade. Many have left off the use of sugar for the purpose of putting a stop to the slave trade. If the custom becomes prevalent of eating and using nothing that slaves have touched, we may soon expect to see people in the state of their first nature, naked in the field, feeding like Nebuchadnezzar upon the grass. What wonders their philanthropy or enthusiasm will produce is unknown.'

Clearly, he was protecting his enslavement industry interests and those of other members of his family. He must have been particularly annoyed by the 1799 Slave Trading Act which decreed that enslaving ships could only trade from Liverpool, London and Bristol.

On his death in 1803 he left a significant fortune to his extended family having had no children of his own. Probate granted on 9th January 1804 revealed that he left:

£1,000 to his sister Mary Rawlinson (equivalent to £86,169 in 2024)
£2,500 to his nephew by marriage, John Ford (the husband of his niece Mary Chorley, in turn, the daughter of his sister Sarah Chorley) (£215,422 in 2024) and
£2,500 to her [Sarah Chorley's] other daughter Sarah, who had married John Walker.

To the two children of his sister Elizabeth Ford, named confusingly John Ford and Ann Barclay, £5,000 (£430,845 in 2024).

To another niece, Mary Hutton Vyvyan, daughter of his brother Thomas Hutton, he left a further £1,000.

£400 in trust to pay the interest to his cousin Dorothy Kenyon (£34,468 in 2024)

His 10 shares in the Lancaster Canal to Abraham Rawlinson Barclay, son of his niece Ann Barclay.

His one-ninth share in Goyave and his moiety of an English estate at Howlin Carr, Co. Durham, in trust to be sold for his residuary legatees. [70]

He left Ellel Hall to his nephew John Ford (the son of his sister Elizabeth).

Despite his no longer being in membership, as his certificate of burial attests, Abraham was buried in the Quaker burial ground in Lancaster and not that of St Mary's Church.

John Rawlinson 1741 – 99

John, Thomas Hutton and Mary's second eldest son, a Merchant of Lancaster, and Mary Heightington took each other in marriage on 29 May 1766 in Durham Wallnook Friends Meeting House. Their marriage certificate and that of his brother Abraham show significant numbers of the members of the Rawlinson, Dillworth and Dodshon families present. John and Mary had three children: Thomas Hutton 1767 – 87, John 1770-70 and John 1771-72. Only Thomas Hutton survived beyond infancy but he died aged 20yrs.[71]

John inherited a part share in the Gouyave plantation on his father's death in 1769 and a third of his father's estate. He already had a sixth share in the family company established by his brother.

As we have seen Melinda Elder lists two John Rawlinsons as Additional Port Commissioners of Lancaster in 1770 – 1773 and 1773 - 1776. They were cousins and had singular Investments in enslaving during their period in office. [72]

In September 1771 Sarah Gibson, a wealthy Lancaster spinster living on Church Street, sold 11 lots of land for building at Head Haugh (or Haw) just south of the then town centre. John acquired lots 5 & 6, on which he built a beautiful house. The house is now known as number 4 High Street.

Richard Gillow drew the plans up for John charging him £1.11sh.06d. He later helped him to move and managed the interior décor. John further extended his property by purchasing land from John Barrow, a Quaker Woollen Merchant and lots 7 & 8 from William Lindow, his relative by marriage to his cousin Abigail Rawlinson, plus more land from his new neighbours Thomas Saul and Robert Tomlinson. All of this enabled him to add counting houses on either side of his house. Each is as large as the house giving a clear indication of the number of clerks he had to employ to keep the accounts for his business.

Photograph: Ann Morgan

He was thus a major property owner in Lancaster as in addition to this estate he owned Haverbreaks House, a property on Nip Hill, Castle Hill and a warehouse on St Georges Quay. [73] All were built on the profit from John's and his father's involvement in the enslaving industry.

In 1779, John, as we have already seen, was disowned by Lancaster Monthly Meeting with his brother Abraham for profiting from Privateering. He was not readmitted. [74]

He died in 1799 and was buried in the burial ground of Lancaster Meeting on the authority of George Barrow. His Will provided for his widow to live in the house for the duration of her life. John Ford, his nephew, inherited on her death in 1811, as their three sons had pre-deceased them. John Ford had already inherited Ellel Hall from Abraham Rawlinson so he now became a significant Lancaster property owner.

✧

Thomas Hutton Rawlinson (Junior) 1752 -77

Thomas, the youngest son of Thomas Hutton and Mary would have also inherited a share in the plantation in the West Indies on his father's death in 1769 when he was 17. There is no evidence that he spent time in the West Indies.

The Monthly Meeting minutes of September 1773 suggest that Thomas Hutton had removed himself from the Hardshaw Monthly Meeting and that the meeting had requested a certificate of removal. [75] This suggests that he was working in Liverpool.

Thomas and Hannah Satterthwaite, the daughter of Thomas & Hannah Satterthwaite, took each other in marriage on 5th June 1776 in the Friends Meeting House in Yealand. The marriage record states that Thomas lived in Liverpool, as does his death record, but there is no information about his time there. [76] He may have been working with his cousin Henry Rawlinson.

Thomas died on 05 March 1777, less than a year after his marriage. He was 25. He is buried in the Burial Ground of Lancaster Meeting. William Dillworth signed the document for Thomas's grave as Clerk to the Quarterly Meeting. The probate record of 1778 classed him as a merchant. [77]

His daughter Mary Hutton Rawlinson was born on 15th April 1777, 6 weeks after his death. [78] Hannah did not remarry.

On 13th August 1799 Mary Hutton Rawlinson resigned her membership.[79] The very next day, she married Sir Vyell Vyvyan, seventh baronet and ten years her senior, at St Mary's Church Lancaster and moved to live in St Mawgan in Meneage Cornwall. How did they meet? She bore eight children, two of whom died in infancy. [80]

John Ford 1762 – 1833

John, the son of Isaac Ford, a Quaker in Hardshaw Meeting and a Manchester Check Manufacturer and Elizabeth Rawlinson (Thomas Hutton and Mary Rawlinson's second daughter) inherited much of the significant wealth of his two uncles, Abraham and John Rawlinson, as well as from his parents. It is interesting to follow this money as far as possible.

John Ford, picture by an unknown artist

Isaac Ford, painted by George Romney

Both are in the ownership of the Lancaster Museum Service

John Ford and Mary Chorley took each other in marriage in 1783 in Huyton. She was 17yrs. They had three children: Sally, born in 1784, who died when 10yrs old; John Chorley, 1786, who died aged just 2 days; John, born on 24th May 1789 in Ellel, died there on 14th March 1819 in his 29th year.[82] John, Mary and their family were clearly living with Abraham Rawlinson MP at Ellel Hall during their married life. We can assume that John was working in Abraham Rawlinson Junior's family company.

Mary died on 7th December 1789 aged 23 at Redmaryle near Prescot Lancashire according to her death certificate. Thus John was left with two young children, one a 6-month-old baby.

In November 1800 John married Mary Lawson at Yealand Meeting House. This second marriage appears to have been a quiet ceremony with only three Quakers signing the certificate of marriage. They had eight children of whom five survived: Elizabeth Sarah (1803), Hutton Rawlinson (1804), Charles Dilworth (1806), Robert Lawson (1809), and Edward (1813). In these children's names we see the names of Lancaster Quakers involved in the enslaving industry.

In 1803, John inherited Ellel Hall on the death of his uncle Abraham along with the sum of £2,500 (£215,422 in 2024). Initially he lived at Ellel Hall but at some time prior to the death of his uncle John in 1811 he moved the family to Yealand Conyers to live in Morecambe Lodge. He left his eldest son John, now aged 25, living at Ellel Hall.

Morecambe Lodge consisted of a mansion with two dwellings in the grounds and is described in histories of the village as one of the two chief residences, Leighton Hall being the other where members of the Gillow family lived. The Gillows had connections to John Ford. His Uncle Abraham's company was their chief importer of the mahogany used in their furniture-making business. He would have known them from his time working in the Rawlinson company. The Ford family attended the Quaker Meeting in Yealand Conyers.

John died in 1833 a rich man by any standards. His money was accrued from the involvement of the Rawlinson family in the enslaving industry. There does not seem to be a record of his Will available but research into the lives of his wife, children and grandchildren makes it clear that it was to them that he left the balance of this money.

The 1841 census of England, Wales and Scotland records Mary and Elizabeth at Morecambe Lodge with five servants.

In the 1851 census Mary is still the head of house. At home with her and her three servants, a Footman, Housemaid and Kitchen Maid are her three unmarried children:
Elizabeth Sarah; Hutton Rawlinson and Charles Dilworth. The men are described as Landed Proprietors; Mary and Elizabeth Sarah are Annuitants; Charles Dilworth is blind; it is not clear how long he had been blind. All are living from their investments.

Ten years on, in 1861, the four members of the household have a Cook, 2 Footmen, 2 House Maids, a Kitchen Maid, an Under Gardener and a Laundress living at the property along with an Agricultural Labourer, his wife and 4 children.

By 1871 Hutton Rawlinson Ford Esq was the head of the family. It is not clear when Mary died. They still had 7 servants. Hutton Rawlinson died in January 1879. Elizabeth Sarah and Charles Dilworth were executors of his Will. Charles Dilworth died in 1880. His sister Elizabeth Sarah was his surviving executor. [83]

John and Mary's son Robert Lawson Ford became a solicitor. He moved to Adel in Leeds and married Hannah Pease in 1838. They lived at Adel Grange with their six children. The eldest, John

Rawlinson Ford, also became a solicitor and a shareholder in the Great Western Railway with his son Gervase Lawson Ford and Charles Frederick Ratcliffe Bretherton, a Leeds chemical manufacturer. Here is an example of monies which were accrued by previous generations from the enslaving industry being invested in the British infrastructure.

In 1862 when the American Civil War began, the Leeds Quaker Meeting set up a fund with the Lancashire Cotton Districts Relief Fund. Robert gave £100 in 1865 (the equivalent to £10,532 in 2024) a significant sum of money. [84]

John and Mary's son Edward settled in Old Park Enfield Middlesex. In 1837 he married Elizabeth H W Lewes. They had four children all of whom went on to live in considerable wealth with five servants to meet their needs. Edward was an author and the census returns 1871 – 1891 record that he was a landowner and became a Justice of the Peace 'living off dividends', in particular his investments in the Great Western Railway. This is another example of how money from the profits of the enslaving industry found its way into British infrastructure.

The two-volume 'Return of Owners of Land 1873', known as the Modern Doomsday, records that Hutton Rawlinson Ford owned Morecambe Lodge with 309 acres, 3 rods and 7 perches in Yealand Conyers having an estimated gross rental value of £226 (equating £20,598 in 2024); Elizabeth Sara and Charles Dilworth Rawlinson each owned 135 acres and 5 rods in Yealand Conyers each with an estimated gross rental value of £57 (£5,195 in 2024). Robert Lawson Ford owned 19 acres and 3 rods in Adel - Cum - Eccup with an estimated gross value of £275 (£25,064 in 2024). The survey excluded London so we do not know what land Edward Ford of Old Park Enfield owned. This return provides evidence of profit inherited from the enslaving industry being used to acquire land.

It was Elizabeth Sarah Ford who bequeathed money to the Lancaster Monthly Meeting to hold in trust. The Trust Property Book records several gifts as follows:

A gift in 1882 of £400 was to be invested in the Furness Railway with interest paid annually, half to pay the stipend of the Master at Wyersdale Quaker School and half the stipend of the Mistress at Yealand Quaker School. Trustees appointed were Thomas and William Barrow of Lancaster. In 1883 A further gift of £400 was also invested for the same purpose. These amounts together equate to £82,102 in 2024.

In 1887 a gift of £1,250 plus £200 was made to Yealand Friends School the total equating to £159,813 in 2024. The first sum to maintain the school was to be invested in the London and Brighton South Coast Railway. The second sum of £100 to pay the stipend of the Mistress at Yealand and £100 to the poorer members of the meeting. This was to be distributed at the discretion of the Trustees William Pickard, William, and Thomas Barrow. [85]

In 1907 – 1909 the Trust investments were transferred to John Rawlinson Ford and John Escolme the then Trustees, the transfer being agreed by the Charity Commission. [86]

This money inherited by the children and grandchildren of John Ford provides clear examples of how money derived from the enslaving industry passed into the British economy to buy land, invest in infrastructure and establish welfare projects (Yealand Friends School & Wyersdale School) and became normalised.

REFERENCES

1. The Letter Book of Benjamin Satterthwaite of Lancaster 1737-1744 - MM Schofield (1960) Page 137
2. www.findmypast.co.uk/parishmarriages England & Wales, Society of Friends (Quaker) 1578 – 1841
3. Lancaster Preparative Meeting Minute Book 06 Nov 1698 – 06 April 1740. Lancaster Central and North Area Quaker Meeting Archive FRL 3/1/1/1
4. www.findmypast.co.uk/parishbaptisms England & Wales, Society of Friends (Quaker) 1578 – 1841
5. The Letter Book of Benjamin Satterthwaite of Lancaster 1737-1744 - MM Schofield (1960) Page 131
6. www.slavevoyages.org/voyages/database
7. www.findmypast.co.uk/parishbaptisms England & Wales, Society of Friends (Quaker) 1578 – 1841
8. The Liverpool Plantation Registers 1744-1773 and 1779-1784, ed. M.M. Schofield and D.J. Pope, ed., Wakefield. 1978
9. 'Shoes and Ships and Sealing Wax; Eighteenth-century Lancashire Exports to the colonies' M.M. Schofield Page 74
10. 'Shoes and Ships and Sealing Wax; Eighteenth-century Lancashire Exports to the colonies' M.M. Schofield Page 81
11. 'Shoes and Ships and Sealing Wax; Eighteenth-century Lancashire Exports to the colonies' M.M. Schofield Page 68
12. The Slave Trade and the Economic Development of Eighteenth-Century Lancaster 1992– Melinda Elder Page 98
13. Lancaster Central & North Area Quaker Meeting Archive FRL2/1/5/72 Disownments.
14. University College London Legacies of British Slavery Database www.ucl.ac.uk/lbs/
15. www.findmypast.co.uk/parishbaptisms/marriages England & Wales, Society of Friends (Quaker) 1578 – 1841
16. Lancaster Central & North Area Quaker Meeting Archive FRL 3/1/1/2 Lancaster Preparative Minutes, 4 May 1740 – 6 Dec 1795.
17. Lancaster Central & North Area Quaker Meeting Archive FRL 2/1/1/8 Lancaster Monthly Meeting Minute Book 02 June 1766 – 07 Aril 1774
18. www.slavevoyages.org/voyages/database
19. University College London Legacies of British Slavery Database www.ucl.ac.uk/lbs/
20. www.findmypast.co.uk/parishbaptisms England & Wales, Society of Friends (Quaker) 1578 – 1841
21. www.findmypast.co.uk/parishbaptisms
22. Lancaster Central & North Area Quaker Meeting Archive FRL 2/1/1/9 Lancaster Monthly Meeting Minute Book 07 Aril 1777 - 07 May 1787
23. Liverpool and the raw cotton trade: Alexey Krichtal - M.A. Thesis, Victoria University of Wellington (2013) pp. 35-36
24. www.findmypast.co.uk/parishbaptisms
25. www.findmypast.co.uk/parishmarriages
26. *London Gazette*, Issue 13416, 15/05/1792, p. 316.
27. University College London Legacies of British Slavery Database www.ucl.ac.uk/lbs/
28. National Archives reference IR27/290

29. www.slavevoyages.org/voyages/database
30. www.findmypast.co.uk/parishbaptisms/marriages England & Wales, Society of Friends (Quaker) 1578 – 1841
31. The Slave Trade and the Economic Development of Eighteenth-Century Lancaster 1992– Melinda Elder Page 182
32. Lancashire Archives Ref: R114a/5
33. www.findmypast.co.uk/education/apprenticeships
34. Provincial Merchants in Eighteenth-Century England: The 'Great Oaks' of Manchester. EHR, CXXXVI. 580 (June 2021) http://creativecommons.org/licenses/by/4.0/
35. www.findmypast.co.uk/parishmarriages England & Wales, Society of Friends (Quaker) 1578 – 1841
36. Manchester Mercury 1795 in www.findmypast.co.uk
37. Lancaster Central & North Area Quaker Meeting Archive FRL 2/1/1/9 Lancaster Monthly Meeting Minute Book 07 Aril 1777 - 07 May 1787 September 1779
38. www.findmypast.co.uk/parishbaptisms/marriages England & Wales, Society of Friends (Quaker) 1578 – 1841
39. The Slave Trade and the Economic Development of Eighteenth-Century Lancaster 1992– Melinda Elder Page 116/7
Lancaster Central & North Area Quaker Meeting Archive FRL 2/1/1/9 Lancaster Monthly Meeting Minute Book 07 Aril 1777 - 07 May 1787 March 1785
40. Lancaster Central & North Area Quaker Meeting Archive Letter FRL 2/1/33/70
41. Lancaster Central & North Area Quaker Meeting Archive Lancaster Preparative Meeting FRL 3/1/1/2 Minutes 04 May 1740 – 06 December 1795
42. Lancaster Central & North Area Quaker Meeting Archive FRL 2/1/1/11 Monthly Meeting Minutes 05 Dec 1790 – 02 Nov 1795
43. University College London Legacies of British Slavery Database www.ucl.ac.uk/lbs/person
44. George Pinckard MD: Notes on the West Indies, Written During the 1796 Expedition under the command of General Sir Ralph Abercromby. (Vol 2 pages 66-6)
45. University College London Legacies of British Slavery Database www.ucl.ac.uk/lbs/. Will: Lancashire Archives, W/RW/K/R512/94
46. Lancaster Central & North Area Quaker Meeting Archive Lancaster Monthly Meeting Disownments FRL/2/1/5/126
47. www.findmypast.co.uk/parishbaptisms/marriages England & Wales, Society of Friends (Quaker) 1578 – 1841
48. Quaker Bankers and their Archives at Barclays Group. https://blog.archiveshub.jisc.ac.uk/2018/08/01/quaker-bankers-and-their-archives-at-barclays-group/
49. www.findmypast.co.uk/parishburials England Deaths & Burials 1538-1991
50. Black Lives Matter and Legacies of Slave Ownership in Lancaster: The Bonds and the Booker Brothers in Guyan - Imogen Tyler 2020
51. University College London Legacies of British Slavery Database. www.ucl.ac.uk/lbs/
52. www.findmypast.co.uk/parishbaptisms/marriages England & Wales, Society of Friends (Quaker) 1578 – 1841
53. The Slave Trade and the Economic Development of Eighteenth-Century Lancaster 1992– Melinda Elder Page 26
54. www.findmypast.co.uk/parishbaptisms/marriages England & Wales, Society of Friends (Quaker) 1578 – 1841

55. www.slavevoyages.org/voyages/database
56. The Slave Trade and the Economic Development of Eighteenth-Century Lancaster 1992– Melinda Elder Page 183
57. Abraham Rawlinson Junior Company & Co account book. Lancaster Reference Library
58. www.findmypast.co.uk/marriages England & Wales, Society of Friends (Quaker) 1578 – 1841
59. The Slave Trade and the Economic Development of Eighteenth-Century Lancaster 1992. Melinda Elder. Page 98
60. www.findmypast.co.uk/burials England & Wales, Society of Friends (Quaker) 1578 – 1841
61. Lancashire Archive DDX 2743/MS4300
62. *Mahogany: The Costs of Luxury in Early America.* Jennifer Anderson (2012) *(Cambridge: Harvard University Press) Page 70*
63. www.findmypast.co.uk/marriages England & Wales, Society of Friends (Quaker) 1578 – 1841
64. www.slavevoyages.org/voyages/database
65. Confidently described by Estate Agents MSW Hewitsons & Great British Life February 2013 but not verified.
66. Lancashire Central & North Area Quaker Meeting Archive ref: FRL 1/1/13 London Yearly Meeting Queries - Quarterly Meeting Minute Book 1776 – 1803
67. Lancashire Central & North Area Quaker Meeting Archive ref: FRL 2/1/1/9 Lancaster Monthly Meeting – Main Meeting Minute Book 07 April 1777 – 07 May 1787
68. Lancashire Parish Clerks online www.lan-opc.org.uk
69. www.historyofparliamentonline.org
70. University College London Legacies of British Slavery Database. www.ucl.ac.uk/lbs/
71. www.findmypast.co.uk/marriages/baptisms/burials England & Wales, Society of Friends (Quaker) 1578 – 1841
72. The Slave Trade and the Economic Development of Eighteenth-Century Lancaster 1992. Melinda Elder. Page 182
73. Melinda Elder – A Georgian Merchant's House in Lancaster: John Rawlinson, a West Indies Trader and Gillow client. 2020
74. Lancashire Central & North Area Quaker Meeting Archive ref: FRL 2/1/1/9 Lancaster Monthly Meeting – Main Meeting Minute Book 07 April 1777 – 07 May 1787. November 1779 meeting.
75. Lancashire Central & North Area Quaker Meeting Archive ref: FRL 2/1/1/9 Lancaster Monthly Meeting – Main Meeting Minute Book 02 June 1766 – 07 April 1774. September 1773 meeting.
76. www.findmypast.co.uk/marriages/burials England & Wales, Society of Friends (Quaker) 1578 – 1841
77. Lancashire Archives – Lancashire Wills and Probate Ref: 498B/75
78. www.findmypast.co.uk/births England & Wales, Society of Friends (Quaker) 1578 – 1841
79. Lancashire Central & North Area Quaker Meeting Archive ref: FRL 2/1/8/1 Notice of the resignation from the Society of Friends of Mary Hutton Rawlinson 13 August 1799
80. www.findmypast.co.uk/marriages/births
81. University College London Legacies of British Slavery Database. www.ucl.ac.uk/lbs/
82. www.findmypast.co.uk/marriages/births/burials
83. www.findmypast.co.uk/marriages/burials/census,land&surveys

84. Elizabeth R. Pafford and John H. P. Pafford - Employer and Employed: Ford, Ayrton & Co. Ltd., Silk Spinners with Worker Participation, Leeds and Low Bentham 1870 -1970.
85. Lancashire Central & North Area Quaker Meeting Archive ref: FRL 1/1/16/1 Trust Property General Pages 49 & 57
86. Lancashire Central & North Area Quaker Meeting Archive ref: FRL 2/1/21/33 Financial Papers

COLONIAL TRADERS

INTRODUCTION

These Quaker Merchants made significant money by trading in goods produced by the enslaved of the West indies and America. They must have been aware of the engagement in the trafficking of the enslaved and their ownership by their contemporaries in the Lancaster Quaker community which played such an important role in their lives. The wealth of these Quakers, also derived from the enslaving industry, helped to build the city, provided work for others and certainly made a contribution to Lancaster Preparative and Lancaster Monthly Meetings in the form of their regular giving.

Henry Coward 1645 -1698

Henry, son of Henry Coward (a freeman), was baptised in St Mary's Church Lancaster in 1645. He became a grocer & ironmonger in Lancaster and a first-generation Lancaster Quaker with John Lawson.

On 24 November 1670, Henry and Ellin Green took each other in marriage in a public assembly, on that occasion, in the house of Richard Cleaton. Prior to the Meeting House being built in 1677 Friends married in the home of a Friend. Henry was well respected by all and people lodged their money with him.

He was the first Clerk of the Lancaster Quaker Meeting. Quaker Meetings were held in his house, 21 Market Street. He provided oversight to Quakers imprisoned in Lancaster Castle for non-payment of tithes, supplying the means to them to have heating, light and food.

As a grocer, it is highly likely that he sold imported sugar, probably obtained locally from John Lawson, and he may have also sold tobacco. Sugar and tobacco were both the products of the labour of the enslaved.

William Stout 1665 – 1752

William Stout 'An engraving from an admirable crayon portrait for the aged Quaker' lent to John Harland (1851) by AB Rowley, a Manchester solicitor.

The son of William Stout, a yeoman of Bolton Holmes, and his wife Elizabeth Dickinson, William was one of seven children. His father died in 1679 when William was sixteen and at school in Lancaster. [1]

During his life time Wiliam kept a record of his life 'written in a small neat hand'.[2]

In 1680, William was apprenticed for 7 years to Henry Coward during which time he became a Quaker. At the end of his apprenticeship he took a shop in Market Street and set himself up as one of the five ironmongers in Lancaster. He sold a wide range of goods including goods imported from the West Indies and America, namely sugar and tobacco, and so was involved in the wider enslaving industry. Initially these goods were purchased during a visit to London in 1688 and shipped back to Lancaster. Regular trips to

London for London Yearly Meeting with his return via Sheffield to buy metal goods kept the shop well supplied.

His sale of tobacco from Virginia increased substantially over the years and he made trips to Liverpool to purchase what he could not get from imports direct to Lancaster. By 1709, tobacco from the plantations in Virginia was his best-selling item. That it was produced by the labour of the enslaved he does not mention in his autobiography.

He became an importer himself investing in importing tobacco, molasses, sugar, cotton (which he called cotton wool) and ginger. Then he added exporting to the West Indies and Virginia, the goods he sent often being handled by Quakers there. He was however only ever a minor participant making little profit on some of what he called 'adventures'.

In 1698 twenty Lancaster Quakers emigrated from Liverpool on the *Britannia* to settle in Pennsylvania as colonialists. William sent goods on the ship that were to remain unsold for a good time as the Lancaster Quaker, George Godsalve, who was to sell them, died on the voyage. When they were eventually sold, William's Factor bought tobacco that was loaded onto thirteen different ships. Seven arrived safely and made a profit. Two were lost at sea and his cargo on five lost money when sold in London. He tells us he lost £70 (£13,668 in 2024) on this 'adventure' after a delay of four years.

In 1698 William also invested as one of six local traders, in a ship called *Employment* being built in Warton. Other Quakers involved included Robert and Joshua Lawson and George Godsalve. Between 1699 and 1702, the ship made four voyages to and from Virginia and Barbados. On the last voyage, it was captured by French privateers and the master was taken hostage. The Mate was allowed to sail it back but it was wrecked off the coast of Fleetwood. Its cargo was saved.

William continued to export and import, sending goods out to Virginia on the *Content* in 1706 and the *Love* in 1707, shipping back tobacco for sale in his shop. In 1707 a cargo returning from Jamaica was captured by a French privateer and taken to Cuba. Undeterred he sent out goods to Barbados on the *Love* in 1715 and in 1720 again on the *Love* to Riga. All made, in his own words, 'little profit'.

In 1708 he, with Robert Lawson (senior), oversaw the rebuilding of the Lancaster Quaker Meeting House to make it large enough to hold General Meetings. During these years, he was a devout Quaker and a central figure in the Lancaster Preparative Meeting. By 1709 he was the Clerk and regularly attended General and London Yearly Meetings. He was well respected in the community in Lancaster, taking on serious responsibilities to support individuals, both Quakers and non-Quakers. His reputation as an honest and trustworthy man caused many Lancaster families to ask him to act as a trustee for their legacies, duties he discharged with diligence despite some causing him to have a great deal of work to resolve the business dealings left by those who died. He describes in some detail more than 30 such instances of trusteeship in his autobiography. In addition, he supported family members and neighbours, examples being the gifting of his house in Penny Street to his niece Ellen when she married in 1731, providing financial support to his brother Leonard and his family and providing materials for neighbours to build premises for their businesses.

He gives us an interesting insight into the trading in sugar. In 1709 he records that

'At this time, not above one-fourth part of the sugar was consumed here, as has been since; and above half the sugar imported into this kingdom was exported to Holland, Germany, and the northern kingdoms…' [3]

William died in 1752 and is buried in the grounds of the Meeting House. In his Will he left £5,000 to his nieces and nephews some of which represented land he inherited. [4] (In 2024 this equates to £911,403). William's 'plain dealing' at the 'market price' and 'not running into debt' clearly paid dividends.

There is no evidence of William being involved in selling enslaved people. He does not mention the words slave or slavery in his autobiography. However, he lived through the early years of enslaving ships leaving Lancaster and the involvement of some of his contemporary Quaker Merchants. He must have known that his imports of tobacco, molasses and 'cotton wool' were produced by the labour of enslaved people. That this was not a concern to him surprises us in the 21st century but he would have been aware that early Quaker emigrants to the New World in the 1690s had enslaved Africans and indentured white servants and that the practice was legal and accepted by British society.

Miles Townson 1692 – 1747

It is not easy to be precise about Miles's parentage. I believe him to be Myles Townson, born the son of John Townson in 1692 and baptised on 19 March 1693 in Hawkshead. The evidence supporting this is that Miles named his only child John and had connections with Thomas Satterthwaite, a Quaker originally from Hawkshead.[5]

Miles Townson was one of three executors of Thomas Satterthwaite senior's Will. This may have been to oversee the property Thomas still owned in Colthouse near Hawkshead when he had moved to Brighouse to marry Mary Ledger. Another executor was John Dillworth. Thus Miles was linked to Friends in Lancaster Meeting through this role as well as his membership of the Society of Friends.

We do not know when Miles made his way from Hawkshead to Lancaster and established himself as a Merchant. Nor is it apparent how he became a merchant in Lancaster but, in 1731/32, he was listed as a Free Burgess of Lancaster as 'Townson Miles of Lancaster, Merchant'. [6]

The first record of his being a Quaker is in 1732 when, on 10th December, he and Mary Satterthwaite, the widow of Thomas Satterthwaite, took each other in marriage at Lancaster Meeting House.

Following his marriage, a seizure of his goods for non-payment of tithe is recorded in the Lancaster Quarterly Meeting Book of Sufferings. The entry also includes a requirement to pay '6s.6d demanded for obligations, offering and obventions *(sic)* by the said priest Fenton (Vicar of Lancaster), it being for his marriage'. Being married in the Meeting House had deprived the Vicar of his fee and he was not going to let that happen! [7]

This marriage made Miles the stepfather to Mary's four children. He took two of the boys, Benjamin and Thomas, into his business. We have already seen that Benjamin Satterthwaite was sent to

Barbados to act as the Factor for the business from November 1737 – June 1738 with Abraham Rawlinson and then as sole representative from December 1739 – January 1741.

Miles and Mary had one son, John Townson, born on 04 December 1735. He died just a year later, December 09, and was buried 10 December 1736 in the yard of Lancaster Meeting House. [8]

In 1737 Miles was the biggest subscriber to the account that maintained the buoy at the 'Shoulder of Lune' marking the entrance to the estuary. He was the treasurer from 1734 – 1746. [9] His stepsons, William and Thomas Satterthwaite, were auditors of the account. Miles' interest in ensuring that ships could deliver cargo from the West Indies and America to Lancaster safely is clearly established.

Melinda Elder, in her book 'The Slave Trade and Economic Development of Eighteenth-Century Lancaster' describes him as an 'important merchant in Lancaster and partner of Robert Lawson of Sunderland Point'. She records that in the 1740s, with his stepson William Satterthwaite, an ironmonger, he owned the *Martha,* a ship involved in the colonial trade. [10] His stepson Benjamin Satterthwaite confirms this in a letter he wrote to Thomas Greenup, an African Captain in Liverpool: 'Since I left your town I have been at my step-father Townson's several times who never offered me a birth though they're going to fit out a vessel to Barbados and another for Antigua.' [11] Although the book makes repeated reference to Miles being involved with the Rawlinsons & Dillworths as well as Robert Lawson no detail is given.

MM Schofield, in his essay on 'Benjamin Satterthwaite's Letter Book 1960', references the Lancaster Freemen and Apprentices Book that provides evidence of these partnerships.

> 5 February 1737 Miles Townson and T. H. Rawlinson, merchants.

> 4 July 1745 Miles Townson, Abraham Rawlinson, T. H. Rawlinson and John Dilworth and Sons.

The Apprentice Book also shows that Miles part owned ships with the Rawlinsons for which they took apprentices.

> 8 November 1739 Miles Townson and Co., owners of the ship *Sarah and Mary.*

> 26 May 1752 Miles Townson and T. H. Rawlinson and Co., owners of the ship *Industry.*

The *Industry* made repeated voyages to Barbados in the 1730s. The *Sarah* traded with Barbados in 1737, also taking 'beef, butter, sundry oats, felt hats, feathers, men's shoes, tallow candles, pewter, snuff, northern cotton, cordage, potatoes, cheese, nuts and grutts (possibly new ale). [12]

Miles had connections outside those of the Quaker community with the Unitarian family Touchet in Manchester who were cotton merchants and manufacturers. They provided goods to be shipped to the West Indies and, in turn, received raw materials for their mills produced by the enslaved in Barbados and the West Indies.

His trading activity clearly demonstrates that he was benefiting from the enslaving industry.

Miles died on 15th October 1747, aged 55. Mary, his widow, died on 8th June 1748. Their deaths are recorded in the Monthly Meeting Quaker Records. [13]

Probate was granted in 1750. In his Will Miles made bequests in money of £605 (the equivalent of £112,442 in 2024) to Mary with bequests to his step sons and the remainder of his fortune divided between his sister and his niece.[14] In 1776 his spinster sister disposed of £1,536 in money (the equivalent of £211,002 in 2024).

Myles Birket 1697 – 1785

Myles was born into a first-generation Quaker family. He was the son of James & Elizabeth Birket of Wood, Cartmel Fell. James is described as a Merchant and was a Free Burgess of Lancaster being admitted in 1722/3.[15]

Myles is described by Benjamin Satterthwaite as his family's competitor in the colonial trade. [16]

Myles and a Quaker named Jane took each other in marriage. I cannot trace the record of their marriage which occurred sometime in the 1720s. They had four children recognised in our Lancaster Quaker Monthly Meeting records: Elizabeth, born in 1727 who in 1753 married Dodshon Foster; James, born in 1730 and who died in 1757; Deborah, born in 1738 and who died a spinster in 1762; and Margaret, born in 1746 and buried in 1751.[17]

Myles traded in the 1730s with Barbados with partners Robert Peel and Henry Sergeant neither of whom were Quakers.[18]

By 1740, he was in partnership with Benjamin Satterthwaite sending goods out to Barbados on the *Hope*. In 1745, he had cargo on the *Ruby* bound for Barbados from Lancaster captained by Benjamin Satterthwaite. When living in Barbados Benjamin regularly sent goods and letters to Myles and sent letters from Myles to his brother James who lived in Antigua.[19]

In 1741, Myles was able to vote for Cholmley Turner MP for West Yorkshire as he had bought freehold in Sedbergh although registered as living in Lancaster at the time. [20] He became wealthy through trading and investing in land and property. He owned Hebblethwaite Hall, Sedbergh which dates back to 1500 and Scarthwaite at Crook of Lune outside Lancaster, both of which he left to his Grandson Robert Foster. These properties were purchased from profits made from trading in goods produced by the enslaved. He was another Lancaster Quaker Merchant involved in the enslaving industry.

In 1746, Myles was also in partnership with Abraham Rawlinson in the Caton Furnace Company but this appears to have been their only business association.

In 1749, with his brother James Birket and Nathaniel Booth and two Dutch Merchants, he registered the *Achilles*. This was a colonial trading ship. [21]

Although there is no evidence in the documentation researched that Myles was a trader in enslaved people, he must have been very aware of the trading of enslaved Africans in Barbados when they were sold, having been sent out from Africa on ships owned by his Quaker Friends.

The fact that his daughter married Dodshon Foster, who was a trafficker of the enslaved, makes it difficult to believe that he had no knowledge of this trade. In 1757, with Dodshon Foster he owned a ship the *Hawke* which sailed between the West Indies and South Carolina but does not appear to have carried enslaved Africans. [22]

The record of his burial in the grounds of Lancaster Quaker Meeting in 1785 crosses out his membership of the Monthly Meeting but I can find no record of his being disowned or his membership being transferred in our archive.

Joshua Whalley 1710 – 1789

Joshua Whalley, a Quaker Grocer from Settle Meeting, and Bridget Dodgson took each other in marriage in Kendal Meeting House on 05 March 1731. Their first children, Jonathan 1734 and Hannah 1735, were born in Settle. However, by the time Abigail was born in 1739 the family were established in Lancaster. [23] The family may have moved in 1736/7 when Joshua was admitted to the Burgess Roll as a Freeman of the city. [24]

As a Quaker Merchant, he took apprentices William Hargreaves in 1744 for a fee of £45 (£9,387 in 2024) and David Dockray in 1748 for a fee of £63 (£11,584 in 2024), the latter being the son of John Dockray, a Quaker of Upperby Cumberland. [25]

He was an executor of Miles Townson's Will in 1750 and both trustee and executor of John Rowlandson's Will in 1769.

His twin sons, Joseph & Caleb, were admitted to the Rolls of the Freemen of the Borough of Lancaster. Their brother Lawson MD was admitted in 1806. [26]

There is no evidence that Joshua was involved in trafficking the enslaved from Africa. As a Grocer he would have been involved in the selling of goods produced by the labour of enslaved Africans thus profiting from the enslaving industry. It was impossible as a Merchant at that time in Lancaster not to be involved as most sold sugar or tobacco nor could they be ignorant of the trafficking taking place out of the port of Lancaster.

David Dockray 1732 – 1807

As we have seen, David was apprenticed by his father to Joshua Whalley, a Lancaster Quaker Grocer in 1748. By 1755, David was a grocer in his own right and was admitted as a Free Burgess. By 1770, he was in partnership with Quakers Thomas and John Dillworth who had engaged in secondary slaving. In this partnership they took on a significant number of apprentices during the 1770 and 1780s. [27] David also invested in a Brewery in Lancaster in 1758 in partnership with Captain John Rowlandson. He was spreading his investments. He was, with Joshua Whalley, an executor of Rowlandson's Will in 1769.

In 1771, he and Ester Dillworth, daughter of William Dillworth and sister to his partners, took each other in marriage at Yealand Meeting House. Ester and David had 9 children: William 1773; John 1775; Thomas 1776; David 1778; Ester 1780; Joseph 1781; Mary 1783; Benjamin 1786; and Hannah 1787. [28]

Lydia Dillworth, Ester's sister, appears to have been present at most of the births. It is interesting that on the Quaker records the women present at a birth are recorded as witnesses to the birth. Ester's father, William Dillworth, Clerk of the Monthly Meeting at the time, signed the document registering his grandson's birth.

David Dockray's position as a Merchant in the community grew to such an extent that he was elected as Port Commissioner seven times between 1767 and 1800. [29] He was a West India Merchant trading goods produced by enslaved people, of that there is no doubt, and he made a good living from it. There is no evidence that he had any involvement with trafficking enslaved Africans or secondary slave trading.

David died in 1807 and is buried in Lancaster Meeting House grounds.

His sons Thomas and David had sufficient funds from their father's business to enter into a partnership in a cotton manufacturing business in Cannon Street, Manchester.
This partnership was dissolved on 30 September 1805 and announced in the London Gazette on 1st October 1805.

That was the year David Junior married Abigail Benson, the daughter of a Liverpool Quaker Merchant. Their marriage certificate tells us that John Field, former Clerk of Lancaster Preparative Meeting, had moved to Liverpool and become a Tea Merchant. The marriage certificate is also signed by David's older brother John, and William Rathbone, one of the Liverpool Quakers who was a strong advocate of abolition.

David Junior went on to become a woollen and cloth manufacturer in Manchester. He is listed in the 1821 Pigot's Directory of Manchester as a Manufacturer of Woollen Cords in Duke Street in Ardwick.

By 1851, David was widowed and had moved to Toxteth Park in Liverpool. In the census of that year, he is described as a Landed Proprietor. [30] He died in 1853.

This family history provides an example of how the money that a Lancaster Merchant accrued from the enslaving industry contributed to the development of the Industrial Revolution in Manchester.

The Barrow Family

There are 17 members of the Barrow family buried with headstones in the grounds of Lancaster Quaker Meeting House. This passage records some of those who were most influential in the Quaker Meeting and the economic life of the city. They must have had an awareness of how involved their contemporaries in the Quaker community in Lancaster were in the trafficking of enslaved Africans and their ownership of plantations and of the minutes of the London Yearly Meeting speaking against this.

Edward Barrow 1682 – 1747

Edward was the son of Thomas Barrow, born on 31st October 1682 in Cartmel. Edward Barrow, a Shipwright of Cartmel, married Mary Thornton (widow) by license on 13th January 1721 at St Oswold's Church Warton.

William Stout wrote of having a sixth share in a ship, *'Employment,'* built in Warton in 1698 for the Colonial Trade. [31] Thus, Edward may have gone from Cartmel to work in an already established shipbuilding yard in Warton.

It is not at all clear when John and Mary became Quakers but his children are all recorded in the Lancaster Quaker Monthly Meeting birth records. Edward and Mary had four children, Thomas 1722; Jane 1724; Edward 1725; and John 1727. [32]

In 1722/3, he was listed as a Free Burgess of Lancaster 'Barrow, Edward, of Silverdale, ship carpenter'. [33] It is likely that he was the owner of a shipyard near Leighton Moss.

Andy Denwood, in an article on shipbuilding near Warton (October 2017), reports that a notebook recording the daily transactions of a tradesman working in the shipbuilding industry in Warton came to light covering the years 1722 to 1727. Although it is unsigned, Dr Nigel Dalziel, a former curator at Lancaster Maritime Museum, believed it to be the work of Edward Barrow. One scribbled sentence on page 8 of the notebook refers to labour provided for work at "kear", which is taken by Dr Dalziel to mean the river Keer in the parish of Warton. Overall, the evidence of the notebook seems to support the idea that ships were being built on the river Keer in the late seventeenth and early eighteenth centuries. It is believed that this took place on the mud flats above high tide level and needed little infrastructure.

Edward died in 1727 aged 45, leaving more than £660 (the equivalent of £112,795 in 2024) as well as "plank at Sunderland", "timber in sundry places" and an eighth share in two ships, *Mary* and *Manchester.* The shares in these ships suggest that he had a significant role in building them. Both ships were likely to have been involved in the colonial trade with the West Indies and John would have had a share in the profit from their sailings. It is highly unlikely that either ship was involved in trafficking enslaved Africans as the first slave ship to leave Lancaster was the *Price Fredrick* in 1736 whose ownership is not known. [34] Several ships of the name Mary sailed from Lancaster – George Chippendale and John Middleton's *Mary* sailed to Barbados throughout the late 1730s, and a slave ship *Mary* of Lancaster was 'cut off by the slaves and most of the people murdered' in 1761 on the coast of Guinea. [35]

Thus, Mary Barrow, although left with four very young children, one newly born, had funds to look after them in the form of an income from her shares in the two ships. At some stage she moved to Lancaster probably to live with her youngest son John. She died in 1769 and is buried in the grounds of Lancaster Meeting House.

John Barrow 1727 – 1795

John Barrow and Abigail Dodgson took each other in marriage on 8 April 1758 at Preston Patrick Friends Meeting House. He had become a Woollen Draper in Lancaster in all probability set up by his mother.

John and Abigail had seven children: Edward 1759; Elizabeth 1761; George 1763; Thomas 1765; John 1767; William 1769; and Jonathan 1770 who only lived 2 weeks. [36]

John was involved in the colonial trade, buying and selling goods produced by the enslaved. In 1749/50, John became a Free Burgess of Lancaster 'Barrow, John, of Lancaster, Mercer'. [37]

In 1763 he took an apprentice, John Mownick, whose family paid a premium of £100.0s.0d. (£16,629 in 2024). [38] This appears to be the only apprentice he engaged probably because his sons were subsequently employed by him.

John was one of the executors of the Will of John Merrick who died in 1774 'a resident in Barbados.' [39] John Merrick was John Barrow's nephew, the son of his sister Jane and a Factor for him in Barbados. John Merrick has a headstone dated 1774 giving his age as 24 in the grounds of Lancaster Quaker Meeting House. Could his body have been transported back from Barbados for burial in a barrel of rum? The death recorded in the Monthly Meeting records notes a death overseas, 'West India …'

We know from Melinda Elder's book that John was part of the consortium with his sons which owned and registered the ship *Abbey* in 1787, a colonial trading ship. His trading activity clearly indicates that he was involved in the wider enslaving industry.

John is buried in the grounds of Lancaster Meeting House.

Edward Barrow 1759 – 1793

John's eldest child. I can find no record of his being apprenticed so I assume that he worked with his father in the woollen drapery business. In 1778/80 he was admitted as a Free Burgess of Lancaster 'Barrow, Edward, son of John, of Lancaster, woollen draper.' [40]

In 1787, along with his father John, brothers George and Thomas and three men from St George's Grenada (James Baillie, Duncan Campbell and Edmund Thornton), he made up a partnership in the *Abbey,* a colonial trade ship sailing out of Lancaster. Thornton, not a Quaker but born in Lancaster and a relative of the three brother's grandmother, was the linkman for his father's involvement in dealing in the enslaved in Barbados. These Lancaster Merchants, if not directly involved in enslaving, were in partnership with those who were and profited from the enslaving industry. Edward died 11 November 1793 unmarried aged 34.

George Barrow 1763 – 1842

George joined his father's Woollen Drapery business in Lancaster becoming a Free Burgess in 1779/80 'Barrow, George, of Lancaster, son of Jno. of Lancaster, woollen draper.' [41] As we have seen he was a partner in the colonial trading ship *Abbey* in 1787.

George, at the age of 33, married Elizabeth Pumphrey on 1st December 1796 at Worcester Friends Meeting House. Elizabeth was the daughter of John, a Glover in Worcester and Candia Pumphrey. They had nine children: John 1797 who married Sarah Cadbury in 1823; Dodgson 1799 - 1822; George 1801 – 1805; Corbyn 1803 - 1866; Candida 1805 -1855 (who married John Cadbury, a widower, in 1832. Her sons George & Richard went on to found the Cadbury Bournville factory and village in 1879); Abigail 1807 – 1818; George 1810 – 1822; Elizabeth 1812 and Hannah 1817 – 1819. [42]

In 1798 George, with his brothers Thomas and William, together with James Ballie of London, Edmund Thornton of Whittington Hall Westmorland and Duncan Campbell of Grenada, registered the ship *Robert* engaged in colonial trading.

George became a wealthy and influential merchant, a mercer, importing expensive textiles, including silks to Lancaster. Thus his trading was not just with the West Indies. It is surprising that he did not join any of the Guilds of Merchants trading in these goods. Some of George's wealth undoubtedly came in part from trading with Barbados and Grenada. Thus, he was involved in supporting the enslaving industry.

It was during this period that he built Bowerham House for his growing family, now one of the more prestigious homes in Lancaster. The reception for his daughter Candida after her marriage to John Cadbury at Lancaster Meeting House on 24th July 1832 was held at Bowerham House.

George was a significant member of the Lancaster Quaker Preparatory Meeting; he was an Elder and the Clerk as his signatures on many death certificates and in the minute books attest.

In 1826, he was a founding member of the Lancaster Banking Co Ltd (1826-1907). It had been established with £300,000 capital in £100 shares. The five founding directors were Leonard Redmayne, George Barrow, John Armstrong Junior, John Fearnside and James Crossfield. John Coulston was appointed as the bank's first manager and the firm traded from the former premises of the failed private bank of Quakers Dillworth, Arthington & Birkett (est. c.1793) in Penny Street. Branches were opened at Chorley and Kirkham but closed after only a few years. More permanent branches at Preston and Ulverston were opened by 1837. [43]

After George's death, the Lancaster Banking Co. purchased the private bank of Gibson, Wilson & Gregson of Kirkby Lonsdale in 1844 and opened branches in Preston (Fishergate) and Barrow in Furness. The Lancaster office moved to Church Street in 1837 where purpose-built premises were opened in 1870. The bank continued to grow its branch network and assumed limited liability in 1896.

In 1907, the bank amalgamated with Manchester & Liverpool District Banking Co. Eventually the bank became part of the Royal Bank of Scotland.

George died in 1842 leaving the sum of £12,000 (£1,137,431 in 2024) to various family members. He provides us with another example of how the profits from involvement in the enslaving industry in the form of goods produced by the enslaved were used to build properties, to establish a bank and, through his Cadbury grandsons, to help establish the chocolate factory and village of Bournville.

John Barrow 1797 – 1866

John, George's eldest son, who married Sarah Cadbury in 1823, also became a wealthy Merchant as well as a cotton spinning mill proprietor as shown in the 1851 census.

That census records him living at 12 King Street in the heart of the city with his wife, two sons and two servants. He is listed as 'Draper, one of two partners employing two apprentices and with his partner owning a cotton spinning business employing 350 hands'. His son Thomas, aged 21, worked in the drapery shop whilst his son John, aged 19, worked in the counting-house of the mill. [44]

The Mill could have been the White Cross Mill, Lancaster's oldest Mill, built in 1802. The Civic Society Leaflet 21 on Lancaster's Canalside Mills suggests that the mill had two owners prior to it being taken over by the Storey family in 1856.

Thus John was reliant on cotton imported from America for at least one of his business operations. That cotton was being picked by the enslaved in America. It was not until 1865 that the enslaved in America were freed. He was thus supporting the enslaving industry.

John, an Elder of the Monthly Meeting, died in 1866.

William Barrow 1769 - 1853

George's younger brother entered the family business and was accepted as a Free Burgess in 1784/5 'Barrow, William, of Lancaster, son of same John of the same place, woollen draper.' [45]

We know that in 1762 he was a registered shareholder in the ship *Robert* with his brothers George and Thomas. He was involved in trading goods produced by enslaved people.

William's business affairs, initially mainly concerned with cotton, were not always smooth running. In July 1785 William Barrow of Lancaster, a merchant, and Hugh Stirrup, a merchant of London with John Shakeshaft, a merchant of London, and Richard Salisbury of Chipping, a cotton manufacturer, purchased Kirk Mill, a corn mill in Chipping, from Richard Dilworth. They converted it to a cotton spinning mill. They not only owned the mill but also 14 acres of land and cottages.

A new waterwheel was erected external to the building. There were 20 spinning frames, with 1,032 spindles installed and machinery for 6 more frames of 48 spindles. Also carding, roving, drawing and other machines. However, the company was declared bankrupt in August 1787 and all was put up for sale. The company which bought it retained it as a spinning mill. [46]

Here we have another member of the Barrow family using cotton picked by the enslaved in a business venture.

By 1851, William was living at Bath House, Bath St., Lancaster, listed as a land proprietor and retired woollen draper. With him lived a nephew, Joseph Whittark, an apprentice tailor in the family business, and his housekeeper. He died unmarried in 1853. [47]

There is no evidence that this family were involved in trading in or owning enslaved Africans but there is no doubt that they traded in goods produced by the enslaved and so were involved in supporting the enslaving industry. The money they accrued in this way built an extensive family home, established two cotton spinning factories, a bank and contributed to the development of the Cadbury factory and Bourneville village.

REFERENCES

1. www.findmypast/births/burials England & Wales, Society of Friends (Quaker) 1578 – 1841
2. Autobiography of William Stout of Lancaster - Wholesale and Retail Grocer and Ironmonger, a member of the Society of Friends. AD 1665 -1752. Edited from the original manuscript by J Harland. www.ForgottenBooks.org
3. Autobiography of William Stout of Lancaster - Wholesale and Retail Grocer and Ironmonger, a member of the Society of Friends. Page 81
4. Will of William Stout. Lancashire Archive Probate Index Archdeaconry of Richmond (1748-1858) Ref: R496a/47
5. www.findmypast/births England & Wales, Society of Friends (Quaker) 1578 – 1841
6. Burgess Roll. Record Society of Lancaster and Cheshire Vol 90 Page 312
7. Lancaster Central & North Area Quaker Meeting Archive: FRL2/1/6/40 Accounts of Sufferings for Tithes
8. www.findmypast/births/burials England & Wales, Society of Friends (Quaker) 1578 – 1841
9. MM Schofield The Letter Book of Benjamin Satterthwaite of Lancaster 1737-1744 1960 Page 129
10. Melinda Elder 'The Slave Trade and Economic Development of Eighteenth- Century Lancaster' Page 26
11. The Letter Book of Benjamin Satterthwaite of Lancaster 1737-1744 - MM Schofield (1960) Page 160
12. Melinda Elder 'The Slave Trade and Economic Development of Eighteenth- Century Lancaster' Page 24
13. www.findmypast/burials England & Wales, Society of Friends (Quaker) 1578 – 1841
14. Lancashire Archive Probate Index Archdeaconry of Richmond (1748-1858) Ref: R100a/50
15. Rolls of the Freemen of the Borough of Lancaster 1688 - 1840 Page 19
16. Melinda Elder 'The Slave Trade and Economic Development of Eighteenth- Century Lancaster' Page 213
17. www.findmypast/baptisms/marriages/burials England & Wales, Society of Friends (Quaker) 1578 – 1841

18. Melinda Elder 'The Slave Trade and Economic Development of Eighteenth- Century Lancaster' Page 27
19. MM Schofield (1960) The Letter Book of Benjamin Satterthwaite of Lancaster 1737-1744 – Page 155
20. *www.findmypast/Yorkshire Poll Book 1741*
21. Liverpool Plantation Registers 4 & 9 February 1750 registration 14 March 1749 *Achilles*.
22. Melinda Elder 'The Slave Trade and Economic Development of Eighteenth- Century Lancaster' Page 128
23. www.findmypast/baptisms/marriages England & Wales, Society of Friends (Quaker) 1578 – 1841
24. Rolls of the Freemen of the Borough of Lancaster 1688 - 1840 Page 339
25. www.findmypast/education&work/apprentices Britain Country Apprentices 1710 -1808
26. Rolls of the Freemen of the Borough of Lancaster 1688 - 1840 Pages 346 & 7 and 368.
27. Melinda Elder 'The Slave Trade and Economic Development of Eighteenth- Century Lancaster' Page 119
28. www.findmypast/marriages/baptisms England & Wales, Society of Friends (Quaker) 1578 – 1841
29. Melinda Elder 'The Slave Trade and Economic Development of Eighteenth- Century Lancaster' Page 119
30. www.findmypast/censusland&surveys
31. Autobiography of William Stout of Lancaster - Wholesale and Retail grocer and Ironmonger, a member of the Society of Friends Page 48
32. www.findmypast/baptisms England & Wales, Society of Friends (Quaker) 1578 – 1841
33. The Record Society of Lancaster & Cheshire – Volume 87 1935 Page 19
34. Edward Barrow - Probate Lancashire Archive reference number: R416A/26. Archdeaconry of Richmond (1533 – 1748) Recordset: Lancashire Wills and Probate 1457 – 1858
35. Melinda Elder 'The Slave Trade and Economic Development of Eighteenth- Century Lancaster' Page 176
36. www.findmypast/marriages/baptisms England & Wales, Society of Friends (Quaker) 1578 – 1841
37. Record Society of Lancashire and Cheshire Volume 87 1935 Page23
38. www.findmypast/education&work/apprentices Britain Country Apprentices 1710 -1808 & National Archives 24f139
39. Melinda Elder 'The Slave Trade and Economic Development of Eighteenth- Century Lancaster' Page 82
40. The Record Society of Lancaster & Cheshire – Volume 87 1935 Page 31
41. The Record Society of Lancashire and Cheshire – Volume 87 1939 Page 32
42. www.findmypast/marriages/baptisms England & Wales, Society of Friends (Quaker) 1578 – 1841
43. www.banking-history.org.uk/record/lancaster-banking-company-limited
44. www.findmypast/censusland&surveys
45. The Record Society of Lancashire and Cheshire – Volume 87 1939 Page 37
46. www. http://kirkmill.org.uk/?s=William+Barrow
47. www.findmypast/censusland&surveys/burials England & Wales, Society of Friends (Quaker) 1578 – 1841,

LANCASTER MONTHLY MEETING

Why did the Lancaster Monthly Meeting not challenge its Members involved in the enslaving industry?

I have searched for evidence of either the Lancaster Preparative or Monthly Meetings questioning or disowning the Friends involved in the trafficking of enslaved Africans and/or the ownership of enslaved people as requested by the London Yearly Meeting in 1761. I have found no evidence that they did anything formally until 1784 when most of those involved had ceased trafficking though some still owned enslaved people on plantations.

In 1784, Yearly Meeting had requested all Monthly Meetings to 'labour' (sic) with Friends involved in the Slave Trade and report to them in 1785.

At the Quarterly Meeting held on 14 July 1784, the Lancaster Representatives were David Dockray and Charles Parker. That meeting minuted:

'…an inquiry to be made in the several Monthly Meetings if any of their members are in any ways concerned with the slave trade. All which are recommended to the Monthly Meeting a report made to the next Quarterly Meeting.' [1]

The September 1784 Lancaster Preparative Meeting Minute 3 reads as follows:

'That an inquiry be made if any of our members be concerned in the slave trade' it was to be reported to the Quarterly Meeting. [2]

The October 1784 Lancaster Preparative Meeting Minutes recorded:

'On considering if any of our members are in any way concerned, we believe Friends of this meeting to be clear. To be reported to Monthly Meeting.'

Yet on the 6th of February 1785 Lancaster Preparative Meeting reported to the Lancaster Monthly Meeting that:

'Report is made: that on inquiry it appears one member of this meeting is concerned with others not of our Profession, in a plantation in the West Indies that came to him by descent, whereon negros are employed, but none concerned that we know of in the importation of them from Africa which is to be reported to Monthly Meeting.' [3]

Interestingly the Friend is not named in this minute. It is true that by 1784, Lancaster Friends still in membership had ceased trafficking the enslaved across the Atlantic. What is clear is that the Monthly Meeting had ignored the earlier London Yearly Meeting minutes. In particular they ignored the 1761 minute requiring Friends owning the enslaved to be disowned. Otherwise this Friend would have no longer been in membership. In 1761, the Lancaster Monthly Meeting minutes were mainly concerned with the 'arming of ships in a war-like manner' and 'joining with others in subscribing to hire substitutes to serve in the militia contrary to our known testimony'. Even in 1785, when the Preparative Meeting identified a Friend involved in owning the enslaved, they did not recommend disownment to the Monthly Meeting.

Was Thomas Rawlinson the Friend mentioned? His siblings and cousins had been disowned or died by 1785 but, as we have seen, he went on to own a 50% share in 6 more plantations with

Thomas Bond by 1799. In fact the extended Rawlinson family owned or part owned 10 plantations across the generations.

Yealand's Preparative Minute book for this period makes no mention of an inquiry being made in the meeting.

In October 1784, the Quarterly Meeting distributed 300 copies of a leaflet 'The Case for our Fellow Creatures - The Oppressed State of the Negros respectfully recommended for the Serious Consideration of the Legislature of Great- Britain by the People called Quakers' provided by London Yearly Meeting.

On the 7th day of the 3rd month of 1785 the Monthly Meeting appointed Dodshon Foster and Joshua Robinson to produce a report on the investigation. In April 1785, the Quarterly Meeting minuted that:

'The result of the inquiry concerning the slave trade to be sent to Yearly Meeting.' [4]

Unfortunately this minute does not record what the result was and a copy of the report is not in the local archive.

We have already seen that the letter dated 1792 in which the Lancaster Preparative Meeting's Clerk John Field was tactfully questioned about Thomas Rawlinson's ownership of enslaved people was either not followed through by the meeting or, if any action was taken, it was not recorded. He was not disowned. He was still in membership at the time of his death.

George Fox, without any dissension, had established what he called 'Gospel Order'. This meant that although each Preparative Meeting exercised autonomy with respect to membership and pastoral care, it was also directly accountable to the superior bodies, the Monthly, Quarterly and Yearly Meetings. [5] It would appear that the Lancaster Preparative Meeting and the Monthly Meeting did not entirely subscribe to this. Otherwise these Lancaster Friends would have been questioned after 1758 about their 'reaping unrighteous profits from the iniquitous trade', and the Rawlinsons who transported and owned enslaved people throughout the 1770s until the 1790s would have been disowned after the 1761 Yearly Meeting Minute.

That Lancaster Friends would not have known of the involvement of these Quaker Merchants is inconceivable. Friends would have been aware of the growth of their wealth. The crews of the ships leaving Lancaster for Africa and onward would have been locally engaged. They would undoubtedly have shared their experiences of working these enslaving ships on their return to Lancaster. In fact all Lancaster Quaker Merchants trading in cotton, tobacco, mahogany and sugar were involved in the enslaving industry.

What is clear is that in the time of the young Quaker church, Friends were concerned with governing aspects of their lives to ensure unity in marriage, apprenticeships, schooling, dress, language, poor relief, non-payment of tithes, refusal of military service, support for those Friends imprisoned and attendance at Meetings for Worship. Today it is incredible to us that Friends were disowned for marriages with non-Quakers, for being married by a priest or for getting into debt, but not for engaging in trafficking and/or owning enslaved Africans on plantations.

It is worth remembering that in this period, the Quaker community membership was much more diverse in terms of social class than today. A good number of Lancaster Preparative Meeting

Members would have been agricultural workers. It is highly unlikely that they would challenge the wealthy merchants, often land owners and employers. Those in significant roles in the Lancaster Quaker Meeting who could have been challenged were drawn from the very group that should have been challenged.

Thus, despite minutes from the London Yearly Meeting asking them to 'labour (sic) with those involved in the slave trade and disown those owning slaves,' Lancaster Preparative and Monthly Meetings were probably not in a position to do so. Such challenges would undoubtedly have caused conflict and they were about ensuring unity in the meeting. Trafficking enslaved people and owning them were very 'weighty matters' as the Quakers of Pennsylvania found when their 1688 Meeting ducked discerning the petition of its Dutch Members 'against the traffic of men-body', as they found the matter 'so weighty that we think it not expedient for us to meddle with it here'. They passed it onwards via their structure to London Yearly Meeting. [6]

Our forebears' actions are seen by us today as immoral and totally lacking in compassion. We do not comprehend the inaction of the Lancaster Quaker Preparative and Monthly Meetings at that time nor of their ignoring the minutes and Testimonies of London Yearly Meeting opposing the enslaving industry. Lancaster had in membership Friends whose involvement in that industry was out of balance with those pronouncements. Their positions as Clerks and Elders in the meetings and employers in the city would have made it difficult to challenge business activities that were accepted as the norm and were, in fact, legal.

The inaction of the Monthly and Preparative Meetings made them complicit in the actions of those in membership who were involved.

The Catholic Church had justified the enslavement of non-Christians in the 15th century and European countries and Merchants had gone along with this. British government loans encouraged ownership of plantations. Enslaving people was a legal activity in Britain until 1807 and the ownership of enslaved people on plantations until 1833 in the British Empire. All merchants in Britain selling sugar, tobacco, mahogany, cocoa and cotton were involved. All were complicit.

Did the Lancaster Quaker Preparative or Monthly Meetings Benefit Financially?

I have looked at whether money was left to the Meeting by those involved in the enslaving industry. I have found no evidence in Wills of money being left to Lancaster Preparative Meeting. Land, property and money were mainly left to close and extended family members with small bequests to servants.

There are exceptions:
- Thomas Hutton Rawlinson's endowment to the Lancaster Friends School for the purchase of books and pamphlets for poor Quaker children. This continued in use by the school till 1910 when the remaining fund was passed to other local education charities.
- Abraham Rawlinson's donation of books for poor Quakers.
- Elizabeth Sarah Ford's donations to Education Trusts for the Friends' Schools at Wyersdale and Yealand to support the School Master and Mistress' salaries and the upkeep of the school buildings.

The rebuilding of Lancaster Meeting House in 1708 to ensure that it was large enough to house the Northern Four Counties General Meetings was funded by collections from the Preparative Meetings in the four counties' Monthly Meetings. They minuted that year:

'A collection be brought of sixty pounds and upwards from each particular meeting that survives to our next general meeting.'

The collections used to build the original Lancaster Meeting House in 1677 include one from the domestic staff at Swarthmoor Hall. The Housekeeper's book 29th October 1678 records donations of £4.10shillings from members of the household 'given towards building Lancaster Meeting House'. There is no evidence of loans being made by wealthy Friends to support either the building or rebuilding.

The Friends involved in the trafficking of enslaved Africans and/or owning them on plantations and those selling the goods produced by enslaved people did make regular contributions to the Lancaster Preparative Meeting and the Lancaster Monthly Meeting as well as making subscriptions to fund-raising requests. This money undoubtedly came from the profits of the enslaving industry in the case of the families whose histories are outlined in previous chapters.

References

1. Lancaster Central & North Area Quaker Meeting Archive: FRL 1/1/1/13
2. LC&NAQM Archive: FRL 3/1/1/2 & 3
3. Lancaster Preparative Meeting Minute Book - Minutes, 4 May 1740 – 6 Dec 1795 Page 194 Lancaster Central & North Area Quaker Meeting Archive: FRL 3/1/1/2
4. Lancaster Central & North Area Quaker Meeting Archive FRL1/1/1/13
5. Testimony of Inequality – Chapter 2 by Elizabeth Cazden in Quakerism in the Atlantic World 1690 – 1830.
6. Stephen Angell - Quakers from Slave Traders to Early Abolitionists - this far by faith. https://www.pbs.org

QUAKERS OUTSIDE LANCASHIRE WHO SUPPLIED THE INDUSTRY

Samuel Galton Senior 1719 – 1799

Samuel Galton senior, a Quaker gun maker, was the son of linen draper John Galton, a Taunton Magdalen Quaker and Sarah Galton. He was originally apprenticed as a 'haberdasher of small wares' in Bristol in 1735. He married Quaker Mary Farmer in 1746 in Bromsgrove and became a partner in her father and brother's gun-making company.[1]

The firm, founded by James Farmer in 1702, nearly crashed after the Lisbon earthquake in 1755. Samuel bought out his father-in-law, taking on a stream of government contracts for the Board of Ordinance. [2] As well as these contracts, he supplied traffickers of enslaved Africans with guns for their ships and small arms to trade for the enslaved. It is highly likely that the guns on the ships owned by the Rawlinsons and other Lancaster Quakers were from this company as they were the main gun makers in the UK and it was a Quaker-owned business.

Samuel himself engaged in trafficking enslaved Africans out of Bristol, as did his brother John (1705 – 1775). Samuel invested in one journey by *Africa* in 1775 when 293 enslaved we taken from New Calabar to St Kitts. 244 survived the voyage. John Galton invested in two slave trading journeys. The first by *Cape Coast* in 1758 trafficked 300 enslaved from Mano & Anomabu in Ghana to Charleston, South Carolina. 262 disembarked. The second, a voyage by *Kingston* in 1760, trafficked 442 enslaved from an unknown port also to Charleston. 361 disembarked, an appalling loss of life.[3]

Samuel was another Quaker who used his considerable wealth to invest in property. His family lived at Duddeston House Ashton outside Birmingham.

Samuel died in 1799 and was buried in the Friends burial ground in Bull Street, Birmingham.

Samuel Galton Junior 1753-1832

Samuel Junior entered the family business in 1770 aged 17. In 1773, he became the manager of the gun works and in 1774 he became an equal partner with his father. In 1777, he married Lucy Barclay from the Scottish branch of the Quaker Barclay family. [4]

Samuel Junior invested in the *Africa,* a Bristol enslaving ship, along with his father.

By the time of the French Revolution Quakers nationally had become concerned about any involvement of Quakers in the production of weapons, the provision of ships and the financing of war. In 1790, the Yearly Meeting Epistle stated:

'If any be concerned in fabricating or selling Instruments of War, let them be treated with in love; and if by this unreclaimed, let them be further dealt with as those we cannot own. And we intreat (sic) that when warlike preparations are making, Friends be watchful lest any be drawn into loans, arming, or letting out their Ships, or Vessels, or otherwise promoting the destruction of the human Species.' [5]

Within two years Samuel Galton Senior and his son were facing intense disapproval, and they were also criticised for their involvement in the enslaving industry, given their guns were used to purchase the enslaved in Africa. When this was raised with Samuel Junior, he retorted that:

'It is the Farmer who sows Barley, – the Brewer who makes it into Beverage, – the Merchant who imports Rum, or the Distiller who makes Spirits; – are they responsible for the Intemperance, the Disease, the Vice, and Misery, which may ensue from their Abuse?' Why should he be held more responsible than those who traded in tobacco, rum, sugar, rice and cotton?' [6]

In 1792, concerns were raised at a Birmingham Preparative Business Meeting about the ethics of accepting subscriptions from Friends whose wealth had been accumulated through the manufacture and trade of guns. This was eventually passed to the Warwickshire North Monthly Meeting for further discernment in Tamworth on 8th March 1795. Friends were appointed to visit the Galtons, father and son:

'Mention having been made at this, and some former sittings, respecting the Case of Samuel Galton and Samuel Galton, jun. Members of this Meeting, who are in the practice of fabricating and selling Instruments of War, concerning which divers opportunities have been had with the Parties, by several Friends, under the Nomination of Overseers, and others, to some Satisfaction; but thinking it proper that they should be further labored (sic) with, respecting the Inconsistency thereof, with our religious principles: We appoint the following Friends to visit them, on behalf of this Meeting, who are desired to make a Report thereof, at a future Monthly Meeting, viz. Sampson Lloyd, Joseph Gibbins, and James Baker together with any other Friends, who are inclined to join them in the Service.'

Following several meetings between the Galtons and Sampson Lloyd, Joseph Gibbins and James Baker, it was reported on the 8th of July 1795 that Samuel Galton senior:

'has relinquished the business & declined receiving any further emolument from it, the minute as far as respects his case is discontinued…'.

Samuel Junior was not prepared to relinquish his profitable business and addressed the Monthly Meeting on 13th January 1796 defending his position. He argued that for over 70 years, his grandfather, uncle and himself, all Quakers, had been involved in the manufacturing of guns, but the Religious Society of Friends had never before discerned, prior to the Yearly Meeting epistle of 1790, that this conflicted with the Society's principles. He also stated that as all his capital was invested in the gun manufacturing business, he was unable to end his involvement in the gun trade until he could find a suitable business to transfer his capital. He ended by stating that he would ignore any action the Society would take against him.

In response to the address, the following month, on 10th February 1796, the Warwickshire North Monthly Meeting concluded that they could not agree with Galton's arguments and decided that the Meeting could no longer accept financial contributions from him while he continued to manufacture weapons. The minutes state:

'…we cannot admit his arguments as substantial & 'tis matter of real concern to us that he shd (sic) attempt to vindicate a practice which we conceive to be inconsistent with our religious principles & this meet[in]g directs the Preparative Mg (sic) of Birmm (sic), not to receive any further collection from him while he continues in the practice of fabricating & selling Instruments of war as a testimony of our disunity therewith.'

Further visits from representatives from the Monthly Meeting could not make Galton change his mind and at the Monthly Meeting on 9th March 1797 the Meeting went a step further:

'This Meeting, therefore, declines to receive any further Collection from him or to admit his attending our Meetings for discipline, as a testimony of our decided disunity with the practice of fabricating & selling Instruments of war.'

In addition to this, the Warwickshire North Monthly Meeting reported the situation to the regional Warwickshire, Staffordshire and Rutland Quarterly Meeting. This meeting appointed John Cash, Thomas Harris, Joseph Burgess, Joseph Seymour and Jeffery Beavington to visit the Warwickshire Monthly Meeting to discuss the Galton case and meet with Samuel Galton junior. On 13th July 1796, it was reported to the Monthly Meeting that Joseph Seymour and Jeffery Beavington, representing the Quarterly Meeting, and other members from the Monthly Meeting had again visited Galton but had still found him unwilling to give up the family business. Friends gave Galton one more chance and again sent members of the Meeting to discuss the issue with him, but he again stood his ground, refusing to compromise his business and confirming he would not give it up. On 19th August 1796, the Meeting came to its final decision:

Warwickshire Monthly Meeting minute book, minute 3, 19th August 1796

'This meeting, therefore, in order for the clearing of our Society from an imputation of a practice so inconsistent as that of fabricating Instruments for the destruction of mankind, thinks it incumbent on us after the great labour that has been bestow[e]d to declare him not in unity with friends, & herby disowns him as a member of our religious society; nevertheless, we sincerely desire he may experience such a conviction of the rectitude of our Principles & a practice correspondent therewith as may induce friends to restore him again into unity with them. Sampson Lloyd & Joseph Gibbins are desired to read to him a copy of this Minute.'

Thus it was the Peace Testimony and not involvement in supplying the traffickers of enslaved Africans with instruments of war which led to Samuel Galton Junior being out of unity and disowned.

True to his word, Samuel continued to attend Meetings for Worship and to continue in the arms trade. Professor Hilary Beckles, in his book 'Britain's Black Debt' states that by the end of the century, Europe was delivering into Africa an annual average of three hundred thousand guns. Samuel Galton junior and his son Samuel Tertius Galton (1783 – 1844), who were still the owners of the main gun-making company in Britain, would have been making a substantial contribution to that figure. [7]

In 1804, he and Samuel Tertius wound up their business in the gun trade and founded a Birmingham Bank with Paul Moon James. They were joined in time by Samuel's other sons, Hubert John Barclay Galton (1789 – 1864) and John Howard Galton (1794 – 1862). [8] Thus, once again, we have an example of a Quaker who has made a profit from the enslaving industry using that profit to open a bank.

Samuel Galton was re-admitted to the Religious Society of Friends.

When he died in 1832 his fortune amounted to £300,000 (the equivalent in 2024 to £28,154,222.) He had property across Britain and shares in infrastructure projects, including canal companies, the East India Company and the Bank of England. This demonstrates a clear link of money generated from the trafficking of enslaved Africans being used to power the Industrial Revolution. He was buried in the Quaker burial ground at Bull St. [9]

John Wakefield 1738–1811

John was the son of Kendal Quakers Roger Wakefield III and Mary Wilson. He began life as a shearman-dyer apprenticed to his father in the mid-1750s. On the death of Roger in 1756, Mary Wakefield carried on what was a substantial business which included finance as well as dyeing. John was taken into partnership with her by 1760. He became the owner of Gatebeck Gunpowder Mill at Sedgwick on the river Bela in 1764. The company trading as Wakefield, Strickland & Co. Gunpowder was not new to the area. It had been used in the many mining operations in the Lake District for centuries.[10]

As the demand for enslaved Africans increased, guns transformed their being gathered for trafficking. There was something of an arms race in the eighteenth century in West Africa with the more militaristic exporting 'nations' constantly seeking to increase their firepower. John's company supplied gunpowder to the traffickers of enslaved Africans through an agent in Liverpool, an ex-slaver captain Gerrard Preston from Lancaster. [11] The gunpowder was so important to the Liverpool slave traders who exchanged small arms and gunpowder for enslaved Africans that it became known as 'Africa or Liverpool Gold.' In 1800, his company supplied the largest amount of gunpowder to the Liverpool traffickers, i.e. 3,112 x 100lb barrels.[12]

His mother married William Dillworth, the widowed Quaker banker from Lancaster, at Preston Patrick Meeting House in October 1770 and John emulated his step-father by establishing a bank in Kendal in 1788. [13] This is the sixth bank established by Quakers identified in this study using profits from the enslaving industry.

John invested in the North of England Turnpike and had 5 ships trading with the West Indies, importing sugar, rum and cotton, possibly for his cotton mill at Burnside. He invested surplus income, becoming a partner in the Common Brewery Company in Kendal and invested in the Leeds/Liverpool Canal and Lancaster/Kendal Canal.
In 1790, he obtained a licence for a second gunpowder mill and this was established at Low Wood, near Haverthwaite, in 1798/99. Over these years, he became, by any measure, a very wealthy man. As his partners died, he bought out their shares, becoming the sole owner of many of the companies, including the gunpowder mills in which he traded as John Wakefield and Sons from 1795.[14]

Kendal Quaker Monthly Meeting established an investigation in May 1804 into John's links through his gunpowder trading to the 'Africa Trade'. William Dillworth Crewdson led the investigation. His mother was the sister of John's stepfather, William Dillworth. John Wakefield would not deny that he sold gunpowder to traders in enslaved Africans. He refused to cease trading with them and to give up his gunpowder business.

This is hardly surprising as, according to his own annual accounts, the capital value of his gunpowder businesses was as follows:

1788	£15,539	equivalent in 2024	£1,963,837
1798	£38,048		£4,098,197
1799	£61,399		£5,878,544
1805	£81,636		£5,919,792
1806	£60,263		£4,533,398
1810	£69,880		£4,599,748

[15]

At the May 1806 Monthly Meeting John Wakefield was disowned:

'because of his regard to his manufacturing of gunpowder for purposes which we deem inconsistent with our Profession'.[16]

The wording of the minute identifying 'purposes' suggests that both the Quaker Peace Testimony and his involvement in the enslaving industry were considered when discerning his disownment.

John recorded his total capital wealth annually. For the year prior to his death in 1811 his accounts showed his total wealth as £209,775 equating £14,202,649 in 2024. [17]

REFERENCES

1. www.findmypast/births/education&work/apprentices/marriages England & Wales, Society of Friends (Quaker) 1578 – 1841
2. London Gazette 1755 issue number 9465
3. www.slavevoyages.org/voyages/database
4. The Galton Family During the Napoleonic Wars – Jenny Uglow from 'In These Times: Living in Britain through Napoleon's Wars, 1793-1815' (Faber & Faber, 2014)
5. Yearly Meeting minute 1790 – Birmingham City Archive ref MS 3101/B/16/2
6. The Galton Family During the Napoleonic Wars – Jenny Uglow from 'In These Times: Living in Britain through Napoleon's Wars, 1793-1815' (Faber & Faber, 2014)
7. Hilary Beckles 'Britain's Black Debt Reparations for Caribbean Slavery and Native Genocide.' Page 103
8. The Galton Papers – Birmingham City Council Archive ref MS 3101
9. www.findmypast/burials England & Wales, Society of Friends (Quaker) 1578 – 1841
10. www.sedgwickparishcouncil.org.uk/a-detailed-history---part-2--the-wakefields-gunpowder-era-in-sedgwick.html
11. https://co-curate.ncl.ac.uk/low-wood-gunpowder-works/
12. The South Lakeland Gunpowder Manufacturing Industry 1764 – 1936 – Robert Vickers B.sc, MA, MCIT May 2003 Table 4 page 53
13. https://prabook.com/web/john.wakefield/2238684
14. The South Lakeland Gunpowder Manufacturing Industry 1764 – 1936 – Robert Vickers B.sc, MA, MCIT May 2003 Table 4 page 81
15. Extract from C. R. O. (K)., WD/WBox 1/ 3- John Wakefield's Balance Account's in Robert Vickers B.sc, MA, MCIT
16. WDFC/F/1 - Minutes of the Monthly Meeting, Society of Friends, Kendal
    C. R. 0. (K), WD/W/Box 113. John Wakefield's 'Balance Accounts', 1781-1810.

WHY IS THIS HISTORY IMPORTANT?

WHY IS THIS HISTORY IMPORTANT?

David Olusoga (Professor of Public History Manchester University) argues that an accurate and shared understanding of an institution's history is not an academic self-indulgence nor a symptom of political correctness. It is critical to understand how they work in the here and now and their future obligations. He goes on to argue that institutions often mask the reality of their chequered pasts and accentuate the heroic. In so doing, they obscure important insights about how power operates within them and what they owe the world.

Quakers are known as leaders of the abolitionist movement which indeed they were. However, this heroic view of the past masks a murkier side of Quaker history which reveals the involvement of some Quaker families in the enslaving industry in its widest interpretation.

The trafficking of enslaved Africans established a right for white people to exploit West Coast Africans, to treat them as inferior and, in the case of Britain, to expand that right to all the African nations it colonised and exploited over the next three centuries, firmly establishing white privilege.

It rooted attitudes of racism in British society which are so embedded today that they are systemic in institutions and thus in structural injustices. This makes it hard for people to recognise them, to accept they exist, to challenge them and to make changes.

It provided wealth to support the development and expansion of the British Industrial Revolution which was the basis of the economy we have in Britain today. In this sample of Lancaster Quaker merchants we see the money accrued from the enslaving industry used to develop five factories, either cotton spinning or manufacturing and the Cadbury factory at Bournville, to develop six banks, some of which over time became the current Barclays Bank and the Royal Bank of Scotland; to invest in the Lancaster Canal; in the Richmond to Lancaster Turnpike and by later generations to invest in railways.

The power that the income from the enslaving industry gave these Lancaster Quaker merchants enabled two, once no longer members of the Society of Friends, to become Members of Parliament and to use that power to speak against abolition.

It is not just a matter of history. It is who we are today. This history has contributed to making our current British society. It was profoundly wrong to trade in people, to traffic them, to steal and exploit their labour and to profit from the goods they were forced to produce. It is we British, including some Quakers, who did this over a period of 300 years from the 17th to 20th century.

Without an understanding of the true history of an organisation, in this case of British Quakers' involvement in the enslaving industry, it is not possible to acknowledge the legacy that history has left. The legacy left by the trafficking of enslaved Africans continues to be felt in the lives of the descendants of the enslaved across the world today and in the countries from which they were trafficked.

Quakers both in Lancaster and nationally have acknowledged this discomforting history and seek to 'consider deeply how the Society of Friends in Britain might make financial and other reparation for our part in the wrongs of the Transatlantic Slave Trade.' (Britain Yearly Meeting 2022 Minute 27; Action: learning uncomfortable lessons and taking forward our witness.)

Appendix 1

Book of Christian discipline of the Religious Society of Friends in Great Britain

Consisting of extracts on doctrine, practice and church government. Epistles and other documents were issued under the sanction of the Yearly Meeting held in London from the first institution in 1672 to the year 1883.

(Including marriage regulations as amended in 1888)

Section VI - slavery and the slave trade

1. It is the sense of this Meeting that the importing, by Friends, of negroes from their native country and relations is not a commendable nor allowed practice and is therefore censored by this meeting – 1727

2. We fervently warn all in profession with us that they be careful to avoid being anyway concerned with reaping the unrighteous profits arising from the iniquitous practice of dealing in negroes and other slaves; whereby, in the original purchase, one man selleth (sic) another, as he doth the beast that perisheth, without any better pretensions to a property in him than that of superior force, in direct violation of the gospel rule which teacheth all to do as they would be done by and to do good unto all; Being the reverse of that covetous disposition which furnisheth encouragement to those poor ignorant people two perpetuate their savage wars in order to supply the demands of this most unnatural traffic, whereby Great numbers of mankind, free by nature, are subjected to inextricable bondage, and which hath often been observed to fill their possessors with haughtiness, tyranny, luxury and barbarity, corrupting the minds and debasing the morals of their children to the unspeakable prejudice of religion and virtue, and to the exclusion of that holy spirit of universal love, meekness and charity, which is the unchangeable nature and glory of true Christianity   1758. P.E.

3. We lament the slow progress in this country of the cause of our fellowmen, the oppressed black people, but we do not despair of its success: and we desire Friends may never suffer the cause to cool in their minds, through the delay which the opposition of interested men have occasioned in this work of Justice and Mercy; but rather be animated to consider that, the longer the opposition remains, the more necessity there is, on the side of righteousness and benevolence, for steadiness, perseverance and continued breathing of spirit to the God and Father of all, who formed of one blood all the families of the earth.
1793 P.E...4, 5, 6, 7, 8, 9, 10

TIMELINE

Pre 1652, Lancaster Merchants were trading with the West Indies in sugar and tobacco. Lancaster had been a trading port since pre-Roman times.

1652 George Fox, founder of the Quaker church visits Lancaster. John Lawson Colonial Merchant owning a Sugar House, becomes the first Lancaster Quaker.

1660 Royal African Company set up to trade along the West Coast of Africa. They traffick enslaved Africans.

1676 George Fox reminds Friends of the human dignity of African slaves after he visits Barbados but does not condemn slavery.

1677 Lancaster Friends' Meeting House built.

1680 Henry Coward appointed Clerk of Lancaster Preparative Meeting.

1684 Lancaster Map and Directory – 1st generation Quaker Merchants listed, including John Lawson, his Sugar House & Still.

1688 Germantown Quaker Meeting Philadelphia's produce 'Petition Against Slavery'. It is eventually sent to the London Yearly Meeting.

1698 20 Lancaster Quakers emigrate to Philadelphia on the *Britannia,* early colonialists. William Stout sends goods on the ship.

1702 The *Employment* commissioned and owned by Quaker Merchants Robert Lawson, Joshua Lawson, William Stout, George Godsalve, plus four non-Quakers, is wrecked off Fleetwood on its return voyage from Barbados, the Captain having been taken hostage by the French.

1708 Rebuilding of Lancaster Friends' Meeting House to enable it to house the four Northern Counties General Meetings.

1711 South Sea Company set up. Robert Lawson (the Elder), son of John Lawson, invests. Its purpose to supply 4,800 slaves each year for 30 years to the Spanish plantations in Central and Southern America.

1720 Sunderland Point Port built by Robert Lawson, Grandson of John Lawson.

1721 Collapse of the South Sea Company. Robert Lawson (the Elder) avoids bankruptcy.

1727 Quakers use the London Yearly Meeting to publicly denounce the slave trade.

1728 Robert Lawson of Sunderland Point declared bankrupt.

1735 Thomas Hutton Rawlinson captains the ship *Industry* on a voyage to Barbados.

1736 Abraham and Thomas Hutton Rawlinson own 8 of the 17 trading vessels returning to Lancaster from the American mainland and West Indies.

1737 Abraham Rawlinson and Benjamin Satterthwaite in Barbados as Factors for the family firm of Rawlinson & Satterthwaite. Benjamin till 1841.

1738 First enslaving ship, *Lambe,* sails from Lancaster for the West Coast of Africa. Registered in London.

1741 Benjamin Satterthwaite disowned for 'marrying out'.

1744 *Phoenix* part owned by Thomas Rawlinson sails to Benin.

Wynstay part owned by Thomas Rawlinson, traffics 102 enslaved from the Gold Coast to the Caribbean.

1749 Robert Gillow and associates employ Benjamin Satterthwaite as their Factor in Barbados,

Clayton (partly owned by Abraham Rawlinson) traffics 275 enslaved from Bonny to Kingston, Jamaica. 223 disembark.

1750 Act of Parliament passed to improve navigation on the river Loyne (Lune), and for the building of a quay or wharf after Lancaster Merchants and ship owners approached Parliament. First meeting of the Port Commission held.

Clayton (partly owned by Abraham Rawlinson) traffics 380 enslaved from Bonny to Barbados. 312 disembark.

Thomas Satterthwaite disowned for 'marrying out'.

1751 Enslaved people sold in Charleston, South Carolina for William Satterthwaite.

Clayton (part owned by Abraham Rawlinson) traffics 310 enslaved from Bonny captured by the Portuguese.

1752 Dodshon Foster and John Heathcote enter the enslaving industry. They commission the *Barlborough* to be built.

Providence leaves Barbados for South Carolina with 'twenty new negros' owned by Abraham and Thomas Hutton Rawlinson, Thomas and William Dillworth, John Rowlandson and Captain Jonathan Nicholson.

1753 *Barlborough* (John Heathcote and Dodshon Foster & Richard Millerson – captain) traffics 116 enslaved people from the Gold Coast to Kingston Jamaica. 101 disembark

1754 Thomas Satterthwaite and Charles Ingham entered the enslaving industry. *Swallow* transports 98 enslaved people from Gambia to Barbados. 77 disembark.

Barlborough (John Heathcote and Dodshon Foster & Richard Millerson – captain) trafficks 164 enslaved people from Africa to Kingston, Jamaica. 140 disembarked.

1755 Eleven enslaving ships leave Lancaster for West Africa, including the *Bold,* in which John Heathcote has shares and which trafficks enslaved people to Bridgetown.

Cato (John Heathcote, William Watson & Miles Barber owners) 288 enslaved people trafficked to Charleston.

1755 Thomas Satterthwaite and Charles Ingham ship enslaved people from Barbados to South Carolina.

1756 Thomas Satterthwaite and Charles Ingham sell the *Swallow* built in 1751 for the enslaving industry at the Sun Inn Lancaster.

Barlborough (John Heathcote and Dodshon Foster & Richard Millerson – captain) traffick 166 enslaved people from Africa to Kingston, Jamaica. 144 disembark.

Bold (John Heathcote & Co; Dodshon Foster) 150 enslaved trafficked from Africa to Bridgetown (number disembarked not known).

Abraham Rawlinson Junior consolidates the family company making his mother and unmarried sister shareholders in the new company.

1757 Meeting for Sufferings expresses concern about the slave trade and asks for previous minutes condemning the trade to be circulated. They find only one minute made in 1727.

Benjamin Satterthwaite sells enslaved people in the West Indies for William Davenport of Liverpool.

1758 London Yearly Meeting minutes that 'Friends should avoid reaping unrighteous profits from the iniquitous practice of dealing in negroes or other slaves.'

John Heathcote dies and Dodshon Foster ceases trafficking the enslaved.

1759 The *Marlborough* (Thomas Satterthwaite & C Ingham) trafficks 200 enslaved people from Gambia to Charleston. 190 disembark.

1760 The *Marlborough* (T. Satterthwaite & C Ingham) trafficks 229 enslaved people from Gambia to Charleston. 196 disembark.

Cato (John Heathcote's descendants – Barber & Wilson) trafficks 400 enslaved from Sierra Leon to Jamaica. 360 disembark.

1761 London Yearly Meeting recommends that any Quakers found to own slaves should be disowned by their religious community.

1763 The *Kerie* taken as a prize from the French by Abraham & Thomas Hutton Rawlinson with William Lindow. Privateering   William Lindow, resident of Grenada, as Factor for the Rawlinsons.

1764 Benjamin Satterthwaite in Liverpool sells a slave for a Liverpool slaver.

Thomas Satterthwaite admits fault in marrying out and is readmitted to membership.

1765 Abraham and Thomas Hutton Rawlinson, with William Lindow, buy the Goyave Sugar Plantation in Grenada.

1766 *Molly* sails from Africa to Jamaica (John Chorley, Abraham Rawlinson Jr., Henry Rawlinson and Moses Benson) and trafficks 328 enslaved people. 300 disembark.

William Lindow registers the *Hobby-Horse,* which clears Grenada for Dominica with 78 enslaved people on board.

1769 The *Sisters* (Thomas Satterthwaite & C Ingham) traffick 128 enslaved people from Gambia to Charleston.

Thomas Hutton Rawlinson's shares in the Goyave Sugar Plantation in Grenada pass to sons Abraham Rawlinson junior and John Rawlinson.

1773 Abraham Rawlinson registers the slaving ship *Lively* in Jamacia with son Henry and nephew Abraham Junior. Capacity to traffic 270 enslaved people.

Sarah (John Rawlinson 4th share) trafficks 148 enslaved from Sierra Leon to Grenada. 131 disembark.

1776 The *Molly* (Henry Rawlinson; cousin Abraham Rawlinson; John Chorley & Moses Benson) trafficks 328 enslaved people to Jamacia.

Abraham Junior, with cousins Henry Rawlinson & John Chorley, buy Maran Estate/Plantation on Grenada.

1779 Abraham and son Thomas Rawlinson, Abraham Rawlinson Junior and brother John visited for Privateering. Abraham and son Thomas apologise. Abraham Junior and John disowned.

John Lawson, great-grandson of John Lawson of St Leonard's Gate, disowned for adultery. Readmitted after acknowledgement of fault.

1780 Abrahan Rawlinson Senior's sons inherit his share of the Goyave Plantation.

Henry Rawlinson and his wife baptised as Anglicans. He becomes MP for Liverpool.

Abraham Rawlinson Junior of Ellel Hall becomes MP for Lancaster.

Thomas Rawlinson & Thomas Bond buy 2 plantations, one on St Vincent and the other on Grenada.

1781 John Lawson disowned again for adultery.

1783 London Yearly Meeting calls for slavery to be abolished throughout the world starting with a petition to Parliament signed by 273 Quakers.

1784 London Yearly Meeting issues the leaflet 'The Case for our Fellow Creatures - The Oppressed State of the Negros respectfully recommended for the Serious Consideration of the Legislature of Great- Britain by the People called Quakers'.

London Yearly Meeting asks Monthly Meetings to 'labour' with Friends owning slaves and send a report.

1785 London Yearly Meeting asks again for a report from Monthly Meetings on Friends involved in the slave trade.

1786 The *Abbey,* owned by Thomas Rawlinson, conveyed 180 enslaved people between St Vincent and Tobago.

Thomas Rawlinson buys shares in plantations in St Vincent & Grenada.

1787 22 May at No2 George Yard London 8 Quakers and 3 Anglicans met to establish The Society for Effecting the Abolition of the Slave Trade.

Henry Lindow Rawlinson, aged 10, inherits 3 plantations and land from William Lindow. Changes his name to Henry Lindow Lindow.

1788 Slave Trade Act limits the number of slaves a ship could carry. Renewed annually.

1791 Robert Foster, Dodshon Foster's son, at the request of William Wilberforce, the abolitionist, gives evidence before the Select Committee of the House of Commons on the Slave Trade.

1792 24 February letter from James Howarth to John Field, Lancaster Quaker Grocer, mentioning that the ownership of slaves by a Lancaster Friend is known to Friends in York.

1793 London Yearly Meeting minutes concern that abolition was taking so long and asks Friends to be steadfast in pursuing it.

1796 Thomas Rawlinson and Thomas Bond borrow £10,000 from the British government under the Grenada and St Vincent loans scheme to buy 3 more plantations.

1799 Slave Trade Act decrees that slaving ships could only sail from Liverpool, London and Bristol.

Fraternite – a prize from the French (Thomas Rawlinson 4th share) trafficks 195 enslaved from New Calabar to Suriname. 181 disembark.

1802 Thomas Rawlinson dies.

Dr George Pickard publishes his observations of the cruelty he witnessed on the plantation Lancaster in Berbrice owned by Thomas Rawlinson and Thomas Bond.

1803 Thomas Rawlinson's heirs inherit the proceeds from the sale of shares in 5 plantations in Grenada, St Vincent and Berbrice. Broom Hall, Berbice, British Guiana not sold on his death.

1807 Britain passes the Abolition of the Slave Trade Act outlawing the British Atlantic Slave Trade.

1821 Quaker abolitionist George Stacey thanks the Quakers in Lancaster and Preston for the money collected for the 'Fund for Promoting the Total Abolition of the Slave Trade.'

1833 Britain passes the Abolition of Slavery Act, ordering a gradual abolition of slavery in all British colonies. Plantation owners in the West Indies receive 20 million pounds in compensation paid for by a government loan.

1836 Henry Lindow Lindow compensated for the slaves he still owns in 1833.

Banker Abraham Rawlinson's descendants compensated for the slaves still owned in 1833.

1845 Lancaster Friends form their own Anti-Slavery Society to support American Friends imprisoned for objecting to slavery.

2015 The Bank of England Debt raised to pay compensation to British slave owners who freed their slaves in 1833 finally repaid.

PORTRAITS

William Stout
'An engraving from an admirable crayon portrait for the aged Quaker' that was lent to John Harland (1851) by A.B. Rowley, Esq., Solicitor, Manchester, along with a handwritten manuscript of Stout's autobiography. This image was downloaded from http:/www.tyldesley.co.uk/2012/08/william-stout-1665-1752.html.

John Ford
A portrait by an unknown artist in the ownership of Lancaster City Museum Service.

Isaac Ford
A portrait by George Romney in the ownership of Lancaster City Museum Service. George Romney, the most fashionable portrait painter of his time, lived and worked in Kendal and then in London.

Dodshon Foster
A portrait by William Tate, a well-known portrait painter, who was born and worked in Liverpool, a port with which Lancastrian merchants like Dodshon Foster had strong connections. Owned by Lancaster City Museum Service.

Benjamin Satterthwaite
Unknown artist. Displayed in the Judges Lodgings Museum Lancaster. Loaned by the family.

John Satterthwaite
Painted by George Romney displayed in the Judge's Lodgings Museum Lancaster. Loaned by the family.

Abraham Rawlinson Senior
Painted by George Romney, this portrait of Abraham Rawlinson of Grassyard Hall, Caton, near Lancaster was commissioned by William Lindow (1726–1786), husband of Abigail Rawlinson (1740–1791), daughter of Abraham and Ellin Rawlinson, shortly after their marriage on 9th December 1771. It was to hang in their new house in Queen Square, Lancaster. It is owned by Lancaster City Museums Service.

Ellin Rawlinson
This portrait is by an unknown artist commissioned by Ellin's daughter, Abigail Lindow. It is owned by Lancaster City Museums Service.

Lydia Rawlinson
Painted by an unknown artist. It is owned by Lancashire Museum Service and is displayed in the Judges Lodgings Museum Lancaster.

Thomas Hutton Rawlinson
An oil on canvas half-length portrait of Thomas Hutton Rawlinson, painted by George Romney (1732-1802).

Mary Rawlinson
Romney also painted the portrait of Thomas' wife, Mary Rawlinson.

These portraits remained with the Walker branch of the family until purchased for the Judge's Lodgings Museum in 2006. The purchase was generously funded by the Heritage Lottery Fund, the MLA/V&A Purchase Grant Fund and the Art Fund. Owned by Lancashire Museum Service.

Abraham Rawlinson, Junior MP
Oil on Canvas painted by George Romney displayed in the Judges Lodgings Museum Lancaster. Owned by Lancashire Museum Service.

Imagined portraits
Frances Elizabeth Johnson, Issac Rawlinson & John Chance are part of the Facing the Past Exhibition at the Judges Lodgings Museum Lancaster. Painted by Lela Harris 2022.

GLOSSARY

QUAKERS

Members of the Religious Society of Friends (of Truth), a religious movement that grew out of the religious, political and philosophical ferment of the mid-1660s. Their guiding principles include a belief in God or the Spirit, Truth, Peace, Simplicity, Equality and Sustainability. Quakers often use the term 'Friend' to denote a fellow Quaker.

LONDON YEARLY MEETING

An annual meeting of Quakers from across Britain – the decision-making body of the Religious Society of Friends. It grew out of the regional meetings held by early Friends. In 1660 Friends from the whole of Britain were invited to attend. Since 1668, some sort of gathering has been held annually, not always in London.

Originally, the meetings were for men only. A Women's Yearly Meeting first met officially in 1784 having been proposed in 1753, following which there were separate meetings for men and women until 1907 when the Women's Yearly Meeting was laid down.

In 1994 London Yearly Meeting became "The Yearly Meeting of the Religious Society of Friends (Quakers) in Britain" known as **Britain Yearly Meeting**.

This annual assembly of the Quaker church in Britain gives Friends the opportunity to gather in worship, explore current concerns and make decisions.

MEETING FOR SUFFERINGS

The part of the Religious Society of Friends which acts as the Yearly Meeting when not in session. Monthly Meetings send representatives to this meeting which meets monthly in London spiritually to discern matters of concern to Friends and make decisions on them.

QUARTERLY MEETING

The Lancashire Quarterly Meeting became the Lancashire & Cheshire Quarterly Meeting in January 1855. This was also divided into men's and women's meetings. In 2011, both became the **Westmoreland General Meeting**.

The Quarterly Meeting governed the Lancaster, Preston, Fylde, Hardshaw (later Hardshaw East & West), Marsden, Swarthmore, and Cheshire Monthly Meetings. In 2022 Westmoreland General Meeting was laid down.

LANCASTER MONTHLY MEETING

The Lancaster Monthly Meeting governed Lancaster, Calder Bridge (Garstang), Preston, Quernmore, Wyresdale and Yealand Preparative Meetings. There were separate business meetings for men and women until the end of the 19th century.

In 2007, this became **Lancaster Central & North Area Quaker Meeting** the legal body with responsibility for Lancaster, Garstang, Yealand, Bailrigg, Chorley and Preston Local Meetings. Chorley meeting has since left this Area Meeting. This meeting is primarily a meeting for church affairs and may forward decisions to the **Meeting for Sufferings**.

PREPARATIVE MEETINGS

The worshipping communities were local to their immediate areas. These had both men's and women's business meetings till the end of the 19th century. Since 2007, they have been known as **Local Meetings.**

MEETINGS FOR WORSHIP

A meeting of Quakers for the purpose of engaging in silent worship generally lasting an hour but in the 18th century could have lasted four hours. Anyone may speak or make some other appropriate contribution. This is known as 'ministry.'

MEETING HOUSE

The term is generally used by Quakers for the buildings where they meet to worship.

QUAKER FAITH & PRACTICE – THE BOOK OF DISCIPLINE OF THE RELIGIOUS SOCIETY OF FRIENDS (QUAKERS)

'Discipline has overtones of enforcement and correction, but its roots lie in ideas of learning and discipleship. Discipline in our yearly meeting consists for the most part of advice and counsel, the encouragement of self-questioning, of hearing each other in humility and love.' *(From the introduction to Quaker Faith and Practice – version 5.)* First issued in 1738 as a manuscript and revised last in 2013, the book contains minutes of meetings, advices & queries and writings constituting advice to Friends collected over the years.

QUERIES

Originally London Yearly Meeting asked representatives from Quarterly Meetings to answer questions. In 1682, there were three concerning:

- the deaths and imprisonment of Friends in their counties
- how Truth had prospered
- how Friends were in peace and unity.

These became six questions in 1694 and were further expanded but always to collect factual information. By 1723, the term used was 'query' instead of 'question', and answering them became more formal. Replies were recorded in minutes. At the 1791 Yearly Meeting, when they were revised, the term 'general advices' was used. Today, the 42 statements are known as **Advices**

& queries and are individually read regularly in Local Meetings during worship over the course of each year.

THE AUTHOR

Ann Morgan MEd

Ann's early career was spent teaching history and sociology. She worked in education, qualification development and training for forty-six years. Brought up in a Methodist/Socialist household she became a Quaker in 1991 at the time of the first Gulf War. Since then, she has served as an Elder, Pastoral Friend, and Local Meeting Clerk.

From 1996 to 2004, she managed the Quaker Peace and Social Witness Vocational Training Project in Lebanon, a peace project.

On moving to Lancaster from Herefordshire, she became, for some time, chair of the board of Trustees of Global Link, an Education Development organisation in Lancaster which also works to settle Asylum Seekers and Refugees, and was a Trustee of the Quaker Tapestry.

Ann represented British Quakers on the European Ecumenical Round Table on the Legacies of Slavery, Colonialism and Racism. She Co-Clerks the Britain Yearly Meeting Trustees' Reparations Working Group and is an Associate Tutor and Elder at Woodbrooke College.

ACKNOWLEDGEMENTS

I am indebted to the research and insights of Dr Melinda Elder, Professors David Olusoga, James Walvin and Imogen Tyler and many others.

I am very grateful for the support and assistance provided by the Lancashire Record Office in putting up with my many requests for documents from the Lancaster Central and North Area Quaker Meeting Archive which they hold and which is catalogued in a different way to their system.

My gratitude also goes to the Lancaster Museums Service and Lancashire Museum Service for allowing the use in this publication of the portraits and other materials from their archive or on display in their museums and to Giles Johnson for the use of the portraits of his Satterthwaite ancestors.

I am indebted to my Ffriend Dr Elizabeth Roberts for her time, regular encouragement and reviewing of an early version of the manuscript.

Many people have helped to put this manuscript into shape. They include George Bachman; Emily Richards and Sarah Greene at UK Books who have been patient about my requests.

Finally, this research and book would not have been possible without the support, encouragement and critical eye of my family whose patience and love over five years enabled me to keep going to produce my first piece of published work.

Index

A

Abbey, 74, 102
Abbey (Barrow), 103
abolished, 13, 16, 125
abolition, 2, 7, 13, 15, 16, 84, 100, 119, 126, 127
Abolition of Slavery Act, 15, 127
Abolition of the Slave Trade Act, 15, 126
Account book, 77, 80, 91
Achilles, (Myles & James Birkett, Nathaniel Booth), 98
Acknowledged Fault', 61
Acknowledgement of Fault, 35
Acknowledgement of misconduct, 61
Admitting their fault, 30
Affirmations Act, 20
Africa, 7, 8, 9, 10, 13, 14, 16, 28, 35, 36, 41, 48, 50, 61, 65, 75, 77, 80, 81, 98, 99, 108, 109, 113, 114, 115, 116, 122, 123, 124, 125
Africa (Samuel Galton Senior and Junior), 113
Africa Trade, 28, 41, 50, 116
Africans, 2, 6, 7, 8, 9, 10, 12, 25, 27, 28, 35, 37, 49, 55, 60, 65, 73, 74, 81, 96, 98, 99, 100, 101, 105, 108, 109, 111, 113, 115, 116, 119, 122
Agricultural workers, 110
America, 7, 9, 12, 13, 16, 20, 31, 32, 44, 79, 91, 94, 97, 104, 122
American Civil War, 88
Ancots Hall, 74
Anglican, 8, 27, 36, 48, 51, 57, 71, 75, 76, 83
Angola, 10
Antigua, 39, 58, 97, 98
Apologise, 30, 125
Apprentice, 19, 35, 48, 55, 60, 102, 105
Apprentices, 19, 41, 51, 62, 97, 106
apprenticeship scheme, 16, 19
Artisans, 19

B

Bahamas, 31
Bailiff of the Customs, 26
balloted, 30, 75
Bank, 9, 16, 51, 77, 116, 119, 127
Bank of England, 9, 16, 116, 127
bankruptcy, 27, 31, 51, 122
baptism, 51, 83
Barbados, 10, 20, 25, 27, 28, 29, 36, 37, 49, 55, 56, 57, 58, 60, 61, 65, 68, 69, 79, 95, 97, 98, 101, 102, 103, 122, 123, 124
Barclay, Robert, 77
Barclays Bank Ltd, 77
Barlborough (John Heathcote & Dodshon Foster), 38
Barlborough Hall, 37
Barrow, Candida, 103
Barrow, George, 16, 85
Barrow, John, 85, 104
Barrow, John (Junior) 104
Barrow, Mary, 101
Barrow, Thomas, 88
Barrow, William, 16, 88, 104

Beads, 10
Beckles, Hilary, 115
Berbice, 76, 126
Binns, Jonathan, 13
Birket Elizabeth, 98
Birket, Elizabeth, 38
Birket, James, 39, 40, 98
Birket, John, 83
Birket, Myles, 40, 44, 98
Birkett, Myles, 65
Birkett, Robert, 51
Birkett, William, 16
Birmingham Bank, 115
Board of Ordinance, 113
Bold (John Heathcote & Dodshon Foster), 36, 38
Bond, John, 15, 76
Bond, Thomas, 14, 75, 76
Bonny, Nigeria, 10, 79
Book of Sufferings, 48, 96
Booker, 14, 15, 17, 77, 90
Booker, Josia, 15
Booth, Nathaniel, 98
Bourneville village, 105
Bowerham House, 103
Bradford, Samuel, 49
Brewery, 99, 116
Brighton South Coast Railway, 88
Britain Yearly Meeting, 11
Britannia, 9, 95, 122
British, 2, 6, 7, 9, 10, 11, 14, 15, 16, 17, 25, 33, 37, 39, 40, 41, 42, 44, 51, 69, 71, 76, 88, 89, 90, 91, 96, 110, 119, 126, 127, 135
British Museum, 25
Broom Hall, 76, 77, 126
Burgess, 20, 27, 28, 29, 30, 32, 35, 37, 48, 55, 60, 96, 98, 99, 101, 102, 103, 104, 105, 115
Burrow, George, 31
Business linkages, 19
Businesses, 9, 44, 95, 116

C

Cadbury factory, 105, 119
Cadbury, John, 103
Cadbury, Richard, 103
Cadbury, Sara, 104
Cadbury, Sarah, 103
Canon Law, 8
Cape Coast (John Galton), 113
Capital flows, 19
Cargo, 20, 36, 44, 57, 58, 59, 79, 95, 97, 98
Caribbean, 9, 16, 25, 70, 79, 117, 123
Cartmel, 101
Cato (John Heathcote, Barber & Wilson), 36, 124
Caton Furnace Company, 98
Certificates of Transfer, 30
Chance, John, 69, 130
Charleston, 32, 33, 37, 55, 58, 59, 61, 113, 123, 124, 125
Chattels, 77
Check Manufacturer, 73, 86

Chorley, Alexander, 80
Chorley, Mary, 84, 86
Chorley, John, 70, 71, 81, 86, 125
Christ Church Oxford, 72
Civil War, 65
Clayton (Abraham Rawlinson), 69
Clerk, 13, 15, 50, 56, 73, 82, 86, 91, 94, 95, 100, 103, 109, 110, 122, 135
Climate change, 16
Coleridge, Samuel Taylor, 40
Colonies, 9, 11, 15, 89, 127
Colonisation, 8, 16
Colonise, 8
Colonising, 9
Colthouse, 48, 96
Commodities, 2, 11, 58
Compensated, 16, 30, 31, 65, 72, 127
Compensation, 16, 73, 77, 127
Complicit, 14, 110
Content (Miles Townson), 57
Content (William Stout), 27
Corporation Act, 19
Cotton, 6, 10, 13, 27, 31, 36, 37, 44, 57, 60, 61, 68, 71, 73, 89, 95, 96, 97, 100, 104, 105, 109, 110, 114, 116, 119
Cotton Mill of Thackray,, 61
Cotton spinning mill, 104
Court of Canterbury, 39
Coward, Henry, 94, 122
Cowrie shells, 10
Crewdson, Thomas, 49
Cromwell, Oliver, 65
Custom House, 13, 38

D

Day, William, 57
Debt, 20, 30, 31, 56, 96, 109
Declaration of Indulgence, 26
Demerara, 37, 76
Dillworth, James, 19
Dillworth, John, 48, 55, 56, 57, 96, 99
Dillworth, John (Junior), 51
Dillworth, Thomas, 49, 50
Dillworth, William, 12, 19, 49, 51, 69, 71, 73, 82, 83, 86, 100, 116, 123
Disown, 29, 110
Disowned, 2, 6, 12, 27, 29, 30, 31, 35, 36, 39, 41, 50, 56, 57, 60, 66, 71, 72, 74, 77, 80, 82, 83, 85, 99, 108, 109, 115, 117, 123, 124, 125
Dockray, David, 49, 99, 100, 108
Dockray, John, 99
Dockray, Thomas, 100
Dockray, David (Junior), 100
Doctrine of Discovery, 8
Dolphin (Robert Foster), 39
Dover, Joseph, 40
Dr Dalziel, 101
Duke of York, 9
Durham, 21, 37, 81, 84

E

Education, 9, 10, 22, 39, 41, 51, 62, 90, 106, 110, 117, 135
Elder, Melinda, 28, 41, 42, 60, 62, 73, 80, 85, 89, 90, 91, 97, 102, 105, 106, 136
Elders, 49, 50, 70, 74, 75, 81, 110
Elizabeth (Robert Lawson of Bristol), 33
Ellel Hall, 81, 83, 84, 85, 87, 125
Ellen & Jane (Abraham Rawlinson), 68
Ellen (Rawlinson), 79
Employment (William Stout), 95
Endeavour (Joshua and John Lawson), 28
Endeavour (Robert Foster), 39
Endowment, 80, 110
Enquiry, 13, 58
Enslave, 8, 10
Enslaved, 2, 6, 7, 8, 9, 10, 11, 12, 13, 14, 16, 22, 25, 26, 27, 28, 29, 30, 31, 32, 35, 36, 37, 38, 39, 40, 41, 44, 48, 49, 50, 55, 57, 58, 59, 60, 61, 65, 69, 71, 72, 73, 74, 75, 76, 77, 79, 81, 83, 94, 96, 97, 98, 99, 100, 101, 102, 104, 105, 108, 109, 110, 111, 113, 114, 115, 116, 119, 122, 123, 124, 125, 126
Enslavement, 6, 7, 8, 10, 11, 12, 13, 40, 41, 44, 77, 79, 84, 110
Enslaving, 6, 7, 9, 10, 11, 12, 13, 14, 15, 16, 20, 21, 22, 26, 28, 29, 31, 32, 33, 35, 36, 37, 38, 39, 40, 44, 48, 49, 50, 55, 58, 59, 60, 61, 65, 66, 68, 69, 70, 72, 73, 74, 75, 79, 81, 84, 85, 87, 88, 94, 96, 97, 98, 99, 100, 102, 103, 104, 105, 108, 109, 110, 111, 113, 114, 115, 116, 117, 119, 123, 124
Enslaving ships, 10, 37, 59, 61, 65, 68, 79, 84, 96, 109, 124
Epistle, 12, 113
Expedition (Thomas Butterfield), 28
Exported, 25, 27, 65, 69, 79, 96

F

Factor, 56, 58, 68, 69, 70, 95, 97, 102, 123, 124
Farmer, James, 113
Fell, Cartmel, 40, 98
Fell, Margaret, 25
Field, John, 15, 50, 75, 76, 100, 109, 126
Flaxman, 48
Fleetwood, 20, 95, 122
Ford, Ann, 77
Ford, Charles Dilworth, 87, 88
Ford, Edward, 88
Ford, Elizabeth, 84
Ford, Elizabeth Sarah, 88, 110
Ford, Hutton Rawlinson, 87, 88
Ford, John, 84, 85, 86, 87, 88, 129
Ford, Robert Lawson, 87, 88
Ford, Isaac, 73, 86
Forge, 65, 68
Foster, Dodgson, 21, 98, 109
Foster, Robert, 37, 39, 98, 126
Fothergill, Alexander, 65
Fountain Estate, 72
Fox, 10, 11, 19, 20, 25, 35, 65, 109, 122
Fox, George, 10, 25
Fraternite (Thomas Rawlinson), 77, 126
Freeman, 48, 99

Friends, 7, 10, 11, 12, 14, 15, 16, 17, 19, 22, 26, 27, 29, 30, 31, 33, 35, 36, 38, 40, 42, 50, 51, 52, 56, 57, 61, 62, 71, 73, 74, 76, 80, 81, 82, 83, 84, 86, 88, 89, 90, 91, 94, 96, 98, 102, 103, 105, 106, 108, 109, 110, 111, 113, 114, 115, 117, 119, 120, 122, 124, 126, 127, 132, 133
Furness Railway, 88

G

Galton, John, 113
Galton, Samuel Junior, 113, 115
Galton, Samuel Senior, 113, 114
Gambia, 10, 55, 59, 60, 61, 123, 124, 125
Gambia (Satterthwaite and Ingman), 60
Gatebeck Gunpowder Mill, 116
General Meeting, 27, 95, 111, 122, 132
George Godsalve, 20, 95, 122
Germantown Quaker Meeting, 11, 122
Gillow, 13, 36, 58, 69, 81, 87, 91, 123
Gillow, Robert, 79, 80
Gilpin, Henry Dilworth, 51
Glasgow, 10, 69
Glasson Dock, 31
God, 10, 11, 14, 20, 21, 120, 132
Gospel Order, 109
Goyave, 68, 70, 71, 75, 80, 84, 125
Grassyard Hall, 68, 71, 72, 129
Great Western Railway, 88
Gregson, William, 69
Grenada, 37, 39, 68, 70, 71, 72, 73, 75, 76, 79, 80, 102, 103, 124, 125, 126
Grocer, 22, 75, 99, 105, 126
Guiana, 76, 126
Gun maker, 113
Gunpowder, 10, 41, 44, 50, 116, 117
Gurney, 77
Gurneys, Birkbeck & Rawlinson Bank, 77

H

Hardshaw, 31, 71, 85, 86, 132
Hawke (Dodshon Foster), 38, 99
Hawkins, John, 9
Hawkshead, 21, 48, 55, 65, 68, 96
Heathcote, Cornelius, 37
Heathcote, John, 19, 21, 35, 36, 37, 38, 41, 44, 60, 123, 124
Heathcote, Millicent, 36
Heathcote, Sir Gilbert, 35, 37
Hebblethwaite, 40, 41, 98
Hebblethwaite Hall, 40
Hodgson, John, 20
Hope (Myles Birket), 98
Howarth, James, 75, 126
human rights, 12

I

Imprisonment, 25, 33, 65, 133
Indentured, 16, 96

Industrial revolution, 6, 10, 22
Industry (Miles Townson), 97
Industry (Rawlinson), 79
Instruments of War, 113, 114
Invested, 6, 9, 27, 28, 44, 66, 80, 88, 95, 99, 113, 114, 116
Invested in land, 80
Investing, 9, 95, 98
Investors, 9, 13, 35, 69
Ironmonger, 22, 33, 55, 105, 106

J

Jamaicans, 16
James II, 9, 26
Jane (Rawlinson), 79
Jepson, William, 15, 49, 71, 83
Johnson, Frances Elizabeth, 59, 130
Judges Lodgings, 80, 129, 130
Jurat, 20

K

Kearton Estate, 72
Kendal, 19, 37, 41, 44, 50, 60, 76, 99, 116, 117, 129
King Alfonso V, 8
King Charles II, 9
Kingston, 35, 36, 59, 69, 123, 124
Kingston (John Galton), 113

L

Labour of the enslaved, 16, 28, 44, 58, 81, 94, 95
Lancaster Banking Co Ltd, 103
Lancaster Castle, 25, 94
Lancaster Maritime Museum, 42, 101
Lancaster Meeting House, 26, 27, 38, 50, 68, 70, 79, 96, 97, 100, 101, 102, 103, 111
Lancaster Port Commission, 38
Lancaster Priory, 77
Lancaster Quakers, 2, 7, 9, 10, 14, 16, 19, 20, 22, 30, 37, 55, 56, 69, 87, 95, 113, 122
Lancaster to Kendal Canal, 44, 116
Lawson, 16, 20, 21, 25, 27, 28, 29, 30, 31, 32, 33, 55, 87, 88, 94, 95, 97, 99, 122, 125
Lawson, Isaac, 32
Lawson, John, 20, 25, 27, 31, 33, 122, 125
Lawson, John (son of Robert the Elder), 27
Lawson, John (son of Robert the Younger), 29, 30
Lawson, Joshua, 20, 31, 122
Lawson, Moss, 29, 32, 33
Lawson, Robert, 44
Lawson, Robert (the Elder), 27, 122
Lawson, Robert (the Younger), 28
Lawson, Robert of Sunderland Point, 31, 32
Legacy, 2, 7, 16, 119
Letter book, 57, 84
Letter of Marque, 12, 70, 82
Letters of Mark, 82
Lindow & Kerie (Abraham & Thomas Hutton Rawlinson), 69

Lindow, William, 44, 68, 69, 70, 72, 73, 80, 85, 124, 125, 126, 129
Lively (Thomas Satterthwaite & Rawlinson family), 50, 60, 68
Liverpool, 9, 10, 13, 15, 30, 37, 50, 55, 57, 58, 59, 60, 62, 69, 70, 71, 72, 76, 79, 81, 84, 85, 86, 89, 95, 97, 100, 103, 106, 116, 124, 125, 126, 129
London Gazette, 20, 22, 32, 51, 52, 89, 100, 117
London Yearly Meeting, 11, 12, 13, 15, 17, 38, 41, 50, 52, 61, 74, 80, 81, 82, 91, 95, 101, 108, 109, 110, 122, 124, 125, 126, 132, 133
Love (William Stout), 95

M

Mahogany, 13, 27, 36, 38, 44, 58, 79, 81, 87, 109, 110
Manchester, 9, 27, 31, 36, 55, 57, 69, 71, 73, 74, 86, 90, 97, 100, 103, 119, 129
Manchester (Mary Barrow), 101
Maran Estate, 71, 125
Market Street, 21, 31, 94
Marlborough (Gilbert Heathcote), 35
Marlborough (Satterthwaite and Ingham), 61
Marquis of Rockingham (Robert Foster), 39
Marry, 9, 20, 57, 96
Marrying out, 27, 30, 36, 58, 60, 123, 125
Martha (Miles Townson), 55
Mary (Mary Barrow), 101
Mary (Miles Townson), 97
Masters, Stuart, 11
Meeting for Sufferings, 11, 12, 15, 49, 50, 124, 132, 133
Meeting for Worship, 10, 26, 56, 57, 61
Memorial stone, 26
Merrick, John, 102
Militia, 12, 30, 33, 75
Militia Act, 30, 33
Millerson, Richard, 35, 38, 123, 124
Minute Books, 19
Minute of Disownment, 12
Minutes, 12, 17, 19, 38, 52, 57, 62, 71, 75, 89, 90, 108, 111, 117
Molasses, 25, 26, 95, 96
Molly (John Chorley Abraham Rawlinson Junior, Henry Rawlinson), 71
Molly (William Watson), 37
Monthly Meeting, 7, 13, 14, 15, 17, 19, 22, 27, 29, 30, 31, 33, 36, 38, 39, 40, 41, 42, 48, 50, 51, 52, 56, 57, 60, 61, 62, 68, 69, 70, 71, 73, 74, 75, 76, 77, 80, 81, 82, 83, 85, 88, 89, 90, 91, 94, 98, 99, 100, 101, 102, 104, 107, 108, 109, 110, 111, 114, 115, 116, 117, 126, 132
Mooreside Burial Ground, 26
Morecambe Lodge, 87, 88
Morley Arthington, Robert, 51
Moss, Isaac, 27, 31
MP, 40, 71, 83, 87, 98, 125, 130

N

nation-wide network, 19
Naylor, James, 65
negros, 14, 49, 57, 69, 75, 80, 108, 123
New Calabar, 10, 113, 126

Newcastle, 41, 70, 73
non-payment of tithes, 94, 109
Nottage, James Barton, 29, 30, 31
Nottage, Mary, 29, 33

O

oath, 19, 25, 26, 28
Olusoga, David, 119, 136
Osnaburghs, 69
Overseer, 39
Overseers, 20, 35, 75, 114

P

Papacy, 8, 9
Papal Bull, 7, 8
Parker, Charles, 76, 108
Penn, William, 9, 35
Pennsylvania, 9, 12, 17, 35, 51, 95, 110
Petition, 11, 12, 13, 110, 125
Petition Against Slavery, 11, 122
Petitions, 15, 84
Philadelphia, 11, 12, 122
Phoenix (Rawlinson), 79
Pickard, George MD, 14, 76
Pickard, William, 88
Pigot's Directory, 100
Plantations, 7, 9, 11, 13, 14, 15, 16, 22, 25, 28, 29, 30, 31, 39, 40, 44, 65, 72, 73, 76, 77, 95, 101, 108, 109, 110, 111, 122, 125, 126
Port Commissioner, 44, 61, 73, 85, 100
Portugal, 7, 8
Portuguese, 7, 8, 9, 69, 123
Preparative Meeting, 12, 16, 31, 39, 41, 45, 50, 68, 71, 72, 75, 76, 89, 90, 95, 100, 108, 109, 110, 111, 122, 132, 133
Preston, 16, 21, 50, 69, 102, 103, 116, 127, 132, 133
Prison, 25, 65, 75
Privateering, 12, 81, 85, 124, 125
Privateers, 39
Prize goods, 81
Probate, 26, 48, 86
Proctor, John, 76
Production of weapons, 113
Providence (Thomas & William Dillworth, Rawlinson), 79
Public buildings, 20

Q

Quaker, 2, 6, 7, 9, 10, 11, 13, 14, 15, 16, 17, 18, 19, 20, 21, 22, 25, 26, 27, 28, 29, 30, 32, 33, 35, 36, 37, 38, 39, 40, 41, 42, 44, 45, 48, 49, 50, 51, 52, 55, 56, 57, 58, 59, 61, 62, 65, 66, 69, 70, 71, 73, 74, 75, 77, 79, 81, 83, 84, 85, 86, 87, 88, 89, 90, 91, 92, 94, 95, 96, 97, 98, 99, 100, 101, 102, 103, 105, 106, 109, 110, 111, 113, 115, 116, 117, 119, 122, 126, 127, 129, 132, 133, 135, 136
Quaker church, 36, 109, 122, 132
Quaker discipline, 20, 58
Quaker Meeting House, 21, 26, 40, 49, 55, 95, 100, 102

Quaker Merchants, 6, 11, 14, 18, 19, 20, 28, 32, 38, 49, 55, 75, 94, 96, 109, 122
Quaker Peace Testimony, 27, 35, 117
Quaker School, 88
Quaker Testimony to Equality, 14
Quaker Testimony to Truth, 7
Quakers Hall, 37
Quarterly Meeting, 19, 22, 26, 48, 50, 75, 76, 82, 86, 91, 96, 108, 109, 115, 132, 133
Quay, 31, 123
Queen Elizabeth I, 9
Queries, 36, 38, 56, 81, 91, 133
Query, 12, 19, 81

R

Racism, 7, 11, 119
Radburn, Nicholas, 2, 13
Rathbone, William, 13
Rawlinson, 14, 27, 29, 43, 44, 48, 50, 51, 55, 56, 60, 63, 65, 68, 69, 70, 71, 72, 75, 76, 77, 79, 80, 82, 83, 84, 85, 86, 87, 88, 91, 97, 98, 108, 109, 110, 122, 123, 124, 125, 126, 127, 129, 130
Rawlinson & Chorley, 70, 71, 79
Rawlinson , Abraham, (Banker), 20
Rawlinson Henry Lindow, 71
Rawlinson John (son of Abraham), 73
Rawlinson John (son of Thomas Hutton), 82, 84
Rawlinson Junior Company & Co, 79, 91
Rawlinson Mary (wife of Thomas Hutton), 84, 86
Rawlinson, Abigail, 44
Rawlinson, Abraham, 15, 69, 76, 83
Rawlinson, Abraham (Junior), 28, 71
Rawlinson, Abraham, Tyzack, 44, 71, 72
Rawlinson, Henry, 65, 71
Rawlinson, Henry Lindow, 44, 72
Rawlinson, Isaac (a negro adult), 83
Rawlinson, John, 88
Rawlinson, Lydia, 74
Rawlinson, Martha, 72
Rawlinson, Samuel, 70
Rawlinson, Thomas, 15, 65, 75, 76
Rawlinson, Thomas Hutton, 20, 49
Rawlinson, Thomas Hutton (Junior), 28, 50
Readmitted, 29, 30, 56, 61, 85, 125
Recovery (John Dillworth), 48
Recovery (Rawlinson), 79
Religious Society of Friends, 17, 26, 60, 66, 83, 114, 115, 120, 132
Report to the Yearly Meeting, 75
Return of Owners of Land, 88
Richard Hubberthorne, 25
Robert (Barrow), 104
Robert (Robert Lawson the Elder), 103
Robert Lawson (the Elder), 33
Robert Lawson of Bristol, 32
Romney, George, 129, 130
Routh, John, 83
Rowntree, John, 29
Royal African Company (RAC), 9

Royal Bank of Scotland, 103, 119
Royal Navy, 39
Ruby (Myles Birket), 98
Rugby School, 72
rum, 25, 26, 36, 60, 102, 114, 116

S

Sally (John Satterthwaite), 59
Sanderson, William, 76
Sarah (John Rawlinson), 125
Sarah (Miles Townson), 97
Sarah (Robert Lawson the Elder), 27
Satterthwaite, Benjamin, 51, 52, 55, 56, 58, 62, 68, 89, 96, 97, 98, 105, 106, 123, 124, 129
Satterthwaite, John, 129
Satterthwaite, Millicent, 35, 41, 44
Satterthwaite, Samuel, 16
Satterthwaite, Thomas, 20, 35, 44, 50, 55, 56, 60, 61, 96, 97, 123, 124, 125
Satterthwaite, William, 16, 44, 55, 56, 97, 123
Scarthwaite Lancaster, 40
Schofield, MM, 51, 52, 55, 61, 62, 69, 89, 97, 105, 106
Sedbergh, 39, 40, 41, 42, 98
Select Committee, 40, 126
Settle, 59, 99
Shiers, Esther, 49
Shiers, Sarah, 49
Shiers, Thomas, 49
Shiers, William, 49
Sierra Leone, 9, 73
Sisters (John Satterthwaite), 59
Slave, 2, 7, 9, 13, 14, 15, 16, 17, 28, 33, 35, 38, 39, 40, 41, 42, 52, 62, 69, 71, 74, 81, 83, 84, 89, 90, 91, 97, 105, 106, 108, 111, 119, 126, 127
Slave Trade Act, 15, 83, 126
Slave Trader Register, 9
Slave-based economies, 11
Slavery, 2, 8, 10, 11, 13, 15, 16, 17, 96, 120, 122, 125, 127
Social standing, 9, 22, 29, 66, 72
South Carolina, 38, 49, 58, 60, 69, 79, 99, 113, 123, 124
South Sea Company, 9, 27, 122
Southern Lake District, 14
Spain, 8, 27
Spanish, 7, 8, 9, 122
Spiritual Lives, 10
St Georges Quay, 85
St John's Church, 71, 83
St Kitts, 59, 113
St Leonards Street, 25, 26
St Mary's Church, 25, 27, 30, 31, 35, 59, 60, 83, 84, 86, 94
St Vincent, 57, 72, 76, 125, 126
St. Georges Quay, 31
Stacey, George, 16, 127
Stag (John Satterthwaite), 59
Stallenge, 19, 20
Steeple-house, 25
Stockdale and Co., 61
Stocks, 25

Storrs, Sarah, 49
Stout, William, 19, 20, 22, 25, 27, 31, 33, 55, 57, 94, 101, 105, 106, 122, 129
Sugar, 9, 13, 25, 26, 27, 35, 36, 44, 57, 58, 60, 68, 70, 76, 84, 94, 95, 96, 99, 109, 110, 114, 116, 122
Sugar House, 20, 25, 26, 28, 122
Sunderland Point Dock, 31
Swallow (Satterthwaite and Ingham), 60
Swarthmoor Hall, 25, 65, 111
Swearing Oaths, 20
Systemic Racism, 7

T

Tenant farmers, 19
Testimony of Denial, 51, 56, 57, 82, 83
The City of Lancaster, 2, 6, 7, 9, 10, 12, 13, 14, 15, 16, 17, 18, 19, 20, 21, 22, 25, 26, 27, 28, 29, 30, 31, 32, 33, 35, 36, 37, 38, 39, 40, 41, 42, 44, 48, 49, 50, 51, 52, 55, 56, 57, 58, 59, 60, 61, 62, 65, 68, 69, 70, 71, 73, 74, 75, 76, 77, 79, 80, 81, 83, 84, 85, 86, 87, 88, 89, 90, 91, 94, 95, 96, 97, 98, 99, 100, 101, 102, 103, 104, 105, 106, 107, 108, 109, 110, 111, 113, 116, 119, 122, 123, 124, 125, 126, 127, 129, 130, 132, 133, 135, 136
The First Publishers, 25
Thomas & John Dowbiggin., 80
Tithe, 48, 96
Tobacco, 13, 27, 44, 94, 95, 96, 99, 109, 110, 114, 122
Townson Miles, 96
Trafficked, 27, 35, 59, 60, 61, 65, 69, 79, 113, 119, 124
Transatlantic Chattel Slave Trade, 7, 11, 13, 16, 27, 61
Transported, 9, 10, 13, 35, 37, 44, 73, 77, 102, 109
Trauma, 16
Trophy Money, 12
Trustee, 135
Trusteeship, 95
Turnpike, 65, 116, 119

U

Unity, 29, 57, 58, 109, 110, 115, 133
University education, 19

V

Valiant Sixty., 65
Virginia, 20, 95
Voyage Book, 69

W

Wakefield, John, 41, 44, 50, 116, 117
Wakefield, Mary, 50, 116
Walvin, James, 10
Warehouse, 38, 85
Warton, 95, 101
Warwickshire Monthly Meeting, 115
Watson, William, 32, 36, 37, 124
Weighty, 12, 15, 50, 82, 110
Welfare Projects, 6
West Africa, 8, 9, 81, 116, 124
West coast of Africa, 9
West Indies, 7, 13, 17, 20, 25, 26, 28, 29, 31, 38, 39, 40, 41, 44, 57, 58, 60, 65, 68, 69, 70, 74, 75, 79, 80, 85, 90, 91, 94, 95, 97, 99, 101, 103, 108, 116, 122, 124, 127
Westbury (Robert Lawson of Bristol), 32
Whalley, Jonathan, 83
Whalley, Joshua, 71
Wharf, 25, 26, 123
White Cross Cotton Mill, 104
White privilege, 7, 119
Whitehaven, 10
Wilberforce, William, 40
Will, 26, 28, 33, 39, 48, 49, 60, 61, 70, 73, 75, 76, 77, 80, 85, 87, 90, 96, 98, 99, 102, 105
William Dillworth (adult negro), 49
Windward Coast, 10
Woollen, 40, 85, 100, 102, 103
Wordsworth, William, 40
Wyersdale, 19, 21, 88, 110
Wynstay (Rawlinson), 79

Y

Yealand Meeting, 19, 51, 87, 100
Yeomen, 19

www.ingramcontent.com/pod-product-compliance
Lightning Source LLC
Chambersburg PA
CBHW040043100526
44583CB00027BA/3263